Self-Directed Groupwork

Self-Directed Groupwork:
Users Take Action for Empowerment

AUDREY MULLENDER & DAVE WARD

Whiting & Birch

LONDON
MCMXCI

Published by Whiting & Birch Ltd, PO Box 872, London SE23 3HL. London 1991

British Library Cataloguing in Publications Data
A CIP catalogue record is available on request from the British Library.

ISBN 1 871177 09 X (casebound)

Printed in Great Britain by Short Run Press, Exeter.

Acknowledgement

This book has grown directly out of the efforts of many groupworkers and group members to find a way of working together that is rooted in anti-oppressive principles. We acknowledge the impact and importance of their work by means of the practice examples we cite throughout the text. The more extended examples are gathered together in an appendix which summarises the groups' activities and also lists where they may be contacted, if they are still in existence and willing for this to happen.

The workers and members of many other groups which have not been listed here have made an equally important contribution to pushing out the boundaries of practice. We wish to acknowledge our great debt to the persevering challenge and innovatory vision of *all* those involved in self-directed action. They have established that groups *can* both set and reach their own goals. We trust that this book does justice to their achievements; if it fails to do so, the responsibility lies, of course, with us as its authors.

Audrey Mullender and Dave Ward

Contents

List of Figures

Dedication

To John

and

to Pam, Anna and Kate,

who empowered us to finish this book.

Foreword

It is with great pleasure and anticipation that we introduce this new groupwork book series, published by Whiting & Birch. As co-editors of the journal GROUPWORK, we are conscious of the exciting and innovative groupwork developments in Britain, Europe and beyond, many of which either do not get published or appear in diverse and relatively inaccessible publications. We hope that the combination of a groupwork journal and book series, both from the same publishing house, will provide groupwork theorists and practitioners with an easily accessible and clearly identified location to turn to for contemporary source material on groupwork.

The purpose of the book series is to provide readers with a diverse range of texts. As with the journal, the central aim is to extend and deepen the body of knowledge and the repertoire of skills needed for groupwork of the highest quality. Our guiding principle is the centrality of the theory/practice relationship, and whilst some publications will be primarily practice-orientated and others more theoretical in emphasis, it is the capacity of theory to inform practice and of practice to be evaluated, conceptualised and contribute to theory which lies at the heart of the series. It is not our intention to promote any one perspective or ideological approach to groupwork, but rather to attract writers who have a well thought out values framework congruent with whatever theoretical/practical approach they are articulating.

Our intention is to include a mixture of single-authored and edited contributions. The latter will provide those readers who are seeking in-depth information on a specialist topic from a range of authors with the material they are looking for readily available in one volume. We shall be delighted to hear from potential authors interested in writing for the series.

The first book in the series is *Self-Directed Groupwork: Users Take Action for Empowerment* by Audrey Mullender & Dave Ward. It is particularly apposite because it epitomises what the series is hoping to achieve. These two authors articulate a model which has its origin in practice and is the product of practitioners and theorists working together over the last decade to develop and refine the model and its value-base. Model-building is a difficult but essential element in the progression of groupwork from an *ad hoc* well-meaning activity to an effective and tested method of practice. Mullender and Ward's text provides a clear and challenging framework for practice which will undoubtedly stimulate all who read it whatever their preferred method and context of practice.

Allan Brown and Andrew Kerslake (Series Editors)

Chapter One

Empowerment:
The Vacuum in Mainstream Practice

A new buzz word has entered the vocabulary of social work - *empowerment* . To be seen as progressive and credible, everyone is trying to jump on the bandwagon. The term creates a vogue image and an aura of moral superiority. In this way, it affords protection against criticism and attack. Yet the term lacks specificity and glosses over significant differences. Rather as happened with the concept of *community* (the vogue word of the 70s but since shorn of some of its magnetism), *empowerment* is 'splattered around by all' (Fine et al., 1985, p.53) and used to justify propositions which, at root, represent varying ideological and political positions. It acts as a 'social aerosol', covering up the disturbing smell of conflict and conceptual division.

Broadly, one finds empowerment publicly associated with two competing concepts. One is the New Right's welfare consumerism (Tonkin, 1988, p.16; Cm 849, 1989) - in effect, the right for those who can afford it to buy choice, amongst whatever services survive Government interference, whilst unpaid carers cope with the rest. The other is the user movement which demands far more, including a voice in controlling standards and services themselves (Kearney and Keenan, 1988, p.3; Brandon and Brandon, 1987 and 1988; Brandon, 1989, p.36). The first is 'the essential expression of individualism' (Heginbotham, 1988, p.24); the second rests on a collective voicing of universal need.

Croft and Beresford (1989b, p.5-6) point out that the user movement is part of a wider philosophy:

> It's also concerned with how we are treated and regarded more generally and with having greater say and control over the whole of our lives. Whatever our age, ethnicity, gender or sexuality we are entitled to be ourselves, be accepted for what we are and not devalued or subject to oppression.

This takes empowerment beyond the manner in which services are provided or help is offered to those in need or in trouble, into a number of reformulations: of the way we see the people we work with; of their own self-image; of the source of these old and new perceptions in the power relationships within our society; and of the nature of oppression.

However one defines empowerment, when it comes to skills and strategies for making it happen in mainstream social work practice, prescriptions are notably lacking. Croft and Beresford (1989a, p.18) see 'three essential dimensions to empowerment': that 'people must be *enabled* to take up opportunities for a say', that 'agencies must offer that say in their own working', and that 'the object of the agency must be an *empowering* one'. They omit a crucial fourth dimension - that ordinary practitioners need a new way of working which, in its foundations, its techniques and its style of operation, empowers those who experience its use. This lack of a suitably empowering methodology has also been evident in the writing of those who chart the radical trends in social work. The edited collection by Langan and Lee (1989), like its predecessors (notably Bailey and Brake, 1975, and Brake and Bailey, 1980) raises key areas of concern for workers rather than telling people how they can make the necessary changes in their everyday practice. It is, of course, always far harder to introduce a satisfactory new way of working than to offer a trenchant critique of the old, as Hudson notes (1985, p.648, though she does give some very valuable 'pointers for change', to use her own phrase).

All of this has created a vacuum which it is our purpose in this book to begin to fill. In this chapter we will offer some initial signposts towards a clearer direction for practitioners and, in the ensuing chapters, we will piece together a more detailed map, in the form of a model of intervention which we have called 'self-directed groupwork' or 'self-directed action'. (The latter indicates that the term covers project and developmental work and campaigning, as well as what is more clearly identifiable as groupwork. The two terms are, largely used interchangeably, however.) At the heart of the model lies a statement of practice principles. These embody an anti-oppressive view of those we work with; a belief that they have the ability to define their own problems, set their own goals and take their own action for change; a commitment to basing this change on broader social analysis than is commonly the case, certainly in most professional intervention; and a style of working in partnership with people which facilitates and empowers them to move in the direction they choose.

Taking a Stand on Empowerment - Confronting Oppression

So what does it mean to empower someone? It has become clear to us, as a result of our explorations into the use of the concept, that by itself the term cannot provide an adequate foundation for practice. The language of empowerment trips too lightly off the tongue and is too easily used merely as a synonym for 'enabling' (Mitchell,1989, p.14). Unless it is accompanied by a commitment to challenging and combating injustice and oppression, which shows itself in actions as well as words, this professional Newspeak (with due acknowledgement to Orwell's *1984*) allows us all, as practitioners, to rewrite accounts of our practice without fundamentally changing the way it is experienced by service users.

As Mitchell has stated for social work (ibid.), we see only one way out of this danger for all related forms of intervention:

> British society is saturated in oppression.... An empowering social work practice derived from such an understanding addresses itself to the powerlessness and loss which results from the material and ideological oppression of black people by white people; working class people by middle class people; women by men; children and old people by 'adults'; disabled people by 'able' people; and gay people by 'straight' people. This social work practice recognises oppression not simply in the behaviours, values and attitudes of individuals and groups, but in institutions, structures, and common sense assumptions.

We begin here to move beyond our own day-to-day work into a wider arena of change. Oppression, unlike such terms as 'poverty', 'deprivation' and 'disadvantage', is not ambiguous as to the exploitative nature of economic and social relationships (Kidd and Kumar, 1981, p.5). Consequently,empowerment, if conected with a notion of oppression couched in these terms, *can* become a distinctive underpinning for practice, and one which does not become colonised or domesticated in the service of the status quo.

However, oppression - if it is to be useful in providing substance to empowerment - must have more precise definitions than mere vigorous rhetoric can provide.

Audrey Mullender & Dave Ward

Defining Our Terms: Oppression

'Oppression' can be understood both as a state of affairs in which life chances are constructed, and as the process by which this state of affairs is created and maintained. We must look for working definitions of both. As a *state of affairs,* oppression is the presumption in favour of men, white people, and other dominant groups, which skews all social relationships and is encoded in their very structure (Fine et al., 1985, p.34). It is not simply the sum of individual attitudes, though it is revealed at the micro level in the nature of personal relations and at the macro level by 'the assignment of privilege in social hierarchies' (ibid., p.35). It grossly impairs the lives of all those whose experiences are constant reminders of their oppressed status, and leaves them only the choice either of adopting the values of the oppressor or of fighting back. So pervasive and powerful is the oppression, however, that, not infrequently, the former happens by default. The role of consciousness raising then becomes crucial in awakening people to their enslavement and in freeing them to choose active opposition in its stead. We will see in more detail how this can work in Chapter Four.

Oppression is also the *process* which creates, maintains and emerges out of this state of affairs: 'Oppression is the process by which groups or individuals with ascribed or achieved power (the oppressors) unjustly limit the lives, experiences and/or opportunities of groups or individuals with less power (the oppressed)' (NCVS, 1989). This definition continues with the assertion that 'Oppression is supported and perpetuated by society's institutions'. Unless it is challenged head-on, such institutionalised support does not need to show itself as overt and direct repression. In a sophisticated society, it is more likely to take on a variety of more subtle forms - moderating and containing conflict and defining what is to be seen as 'normal' and 'acceptable' through, for example, the workings of the law, the media and the educational system.

What is more, the various forms of oppression are entwined together and must be understood and confronted together. To do otherwise, is to allow one oppressed group to be played off against another in an invidious hierarchy which subverts into fruitless comparisons the energy which should be used in challenging the maintenance of injustice. The fight cannot purely be waged against racism or any other single '-ism':

Oppression can occur along any number of dimensions. Oppression on the basis of class, race, gender, disability, age and sexual orientation is central to our present society which is permeated by relations of domination and subordination. Individuals experiencing oppression through a number of these dimensions experience them simultaneously, not one by one.... The anti-racist struggle is a struggle for equality for all people regardless of their status in society. (Dominelli, 1988, pp.158-159)

It well suits the vested interests of those who benefit from oppression to see the effectiveness of those who would oppose it diluted and neutralised by competing claims to the position of 'most oppressed'. We must be on our guard for attempts to lead the debate in that direction:

it is important to stress the importance of refusing to collude with the establishment of a hierarchy of more or less 'worthy' oppressions. Such a hierarchy enables those in power to pitch one set of political rights and demands against others. (Hudson, 1989, p.25)

Power

According to Lukes (1974), such ploys are a classic manifestation of power because power is the capacity not only to impose one's will, if necessary against the will of other parties, but also to set the terms of the argument, including at the national and international level. A good example of this has been the repackaging of public ills under the guise of private troubles (Wright Mills,1970) by three consecutive Thatcher governments. Thus, social explanations of offending have given way to a stress on personal culpability in criminal justice policies (though the struggle to reverse this trend is well illustrated in Chapter Five); changes in benefits have signalled to individuals that they must ultimately be prepared to provide for themselves or to beg for charity as 'deserving cases'; and the welfare of the poorest and weakest sections of the population has been attacked in hard financial terms, as well as through cut-backs in the provision of services, thus threatening to leave people so preoccupied by the suffering of their own families that they have neither the strength nor the motivation to band together in opposition. The same attempt to individualise all arguments lies behind the official preference for 'consumerism' over user movements which we noted at the beginning of this chapter. All aspects of social change can be conceptualised in these conflicting ways. The very contradiction between them may help us to see both more clearly: as the two sides of a struggle over whether the privileged can hang on to the power with which they oppress others for their own advantage.

Though its effect is gross, the exercise of power, as Lukes argues, may be hidden and subtle, not least in the way it is embedded in our expectations and perceptions. This is why we offer a model which empowers service users by enabling them to look behind the smoke-screens and to perceive power for what it is. (See Chapter Four particularly: 'asking the question WHY'.)

To Confront Oppression We Must First Confront Power

Thus, empowerment as we will refer to it throughout this book is committed in its politics. It recognises that the response to what may appear personal has to be highly political. This is unsurprising and inevitable, since so long as society is differentiated along race, gender and other lines, politics pervade all of social life - including social work and related forms of paid and unpaid intervention (Goldberg and Elliott, 1980, p.478).

Empowering practice, like the demands of the user movements it serves, seeks change not only through *winning* power—bringing to those who have been oppressed the exercise of control over what happens to them - but through transforming it. Just as oppression is experienced through personal and everyday events so, equally, an empowering practice can offer people the chance to try out and experience new ways of being involved in those events at the everyday level. This is the overall aim of our model of action. It looks to share power between workers and participants and to challenge them both to use it non-oppressively. Together, they can construct tentative models for more human forms of social relations which provide in microcosm what is ultimately aspired to at the level of total society.

In this way, even though we are raising the broad questions of power and oppression which so often disable the mainstream practitioner because he or she sees no way of tackling them at the level of day-to-day practice, we are also offering an approach which means they *can* be tackled. Service users themselves are helped to analyse, confront and transform the exercise of power, on a small and localised scale at first but with the capacity to grow from there, since the analysis need not be unsophisticated. This will emerge clearly from the practice examples we give, particularly in Chapters Five and Six.

Action for Change

An understanding of oppression and power, then, is what draws empowerment away from the meaninglessness which otherwise afflicts and devalues the term, and the focus provided by self-directed action prevents all three terms from disappearing into a terrifying breadth of scope. Practitioners can move from the inaction of endless conceptualisation into facilitating real change amongst groups of service users, without requiring superhuman skills or inexhaustible resources. There have been a good many texts which highlight the agenda for change (e.g. Parton, 1985; Frost and Stein, 1989; Pitts, 1990) but none which indicates in sufficient detail how practitioners can engage with it. Self-directed action, in contrast, is not purely an analytical process; it has an active element which gives both users and workers real indications of a way forward.

There are, of course, other forms of progressive practice which have actively confronted oppression and the power that holds it in place. Feminists have, for example, developed forms of consciousness raising as a means both to conceptualise and to tackle individual and organisational sexism. Black activists have reached their own conclusions about ways to promote change and there have also been pockets of activity amongst white workers who accept the responsibility for making fundamental shifts in confronting their own and others' racism.

Until now, however, the impact of such developments has been limited by two major factors. Firstly, they have tended to be confined to fairly narrow areas, remaining on the edges of mainstream professional practice. Secondly, they have been colonised by those who win reflected glory from adopting the terminology without the pain of confronting their own oppressive attitudes at a level deep enough to root them out.

The Frustrations Confronting Feminist Practice ...

Both limitations can be clearly observed in accounts by feminist writers. In 1985, Hudson (pp.635-636) argued that feminist perspectives had the potential to contribute far more to social work (and, one might add, other professional) practice than the

7

'incremental and patchy' picture she saw around her. Since then, two major explorations of the issues surrounding women and social work have appeared (Hanmer and Statham,1988; Dominelli and McLeod,1989) but practice continues to progress at a regrettably slow rate. Even now, there remains much work to be done in conceptualising the detailed implications of gender-informed approaches for empowering intervention (Wise, 1986, p.ii). After all, the canvas is vast and the traditions to be challenged daunting in their scope and smugness. As a woman student riposted to a male class-mate who enquired where the counter-arguments were to a feminist line being presented by the tutor: 'Just read the whole of the rest of social work literature!'

Even where there is a gloss of accepting anti-sexism as an essential prerequisite of empowerment, there may be a failure to dig deeply enough into the old assumptions: 'Radical social work writers have largely "added in" feminist ideas and issues relating to gender, rather than fully integrating feminist perspectives into what are usually explicitly Marxist paradigms' (Hudson, 1985, p.639). If we are to rethink practice from a feminist perspective, we have to recognise that patriarchy is as polluting as capitalism. By developing 'a theory of power rather than of the state' (Rojek et al., 1988, p.99), patriarchy, racism, and other forms of oppression can be revealed as significant factors.

... And Anti-Racist Practice.

The history of anti-racism is certainly one of active struggle and not just of analysis through raised consciousness. Sivanandan (1982) documents how struggle and direct action has been a constant theme for black people, providing a link between earlier anti-colonial struggles in the Empire with those still continuing in Britain today, but gradually resolving itself into 'a more holistic, albeit shifting, pattern of black unity and black struggle' (p.116). Because this struggle confronts, as Dominelli (1989, p.13) puts it, the 'razor-sharp' edge of oppression in the form of racism, it contributes a new clarity of analysis, and a commitment to real and concrete action for change'.

It has been marginalised by many factors, however. For black women, there has been the frustration of being left out of account by those white feminists who fail to see the importance of a combined struggle:

Black feminists have focused in particular on the way white feminists' presumptions about the 'intrinsic oppression' of the family have denied both the impact of racism on black families and the role of the family as a bulwark against a racist world . . . . Racism and sexism . . . have different historical roots; their consequences are also generally dissimilar. (Hudson,1989, pp.74-75)

Black women have been left to fight alone and have had to make their own connections (Bryan et al., 1985). Foster-Carter (1987, p.53) shows how black women have fought back, organising themselves without support from existing movements, not borrowing theories and practices but making the struggle relevant to their own experiences. She acknowledges the interlocking dimensions of their oppression - racial oppression, sexual domination and class - but emphasises how 'a common experience as second class citizens in contemporary Britain' (ibid., p.47), an experience which is specifically black and structured by racism, provided the basis for solidarity and collective action.

Workers - even, sometimes, black workers because of their socialisation into white agencies - have to learn to recognise and work with these strengths. In this context, Tara Mistry, a black probation officer, vividly describes what she and the white participants learned from the black members of a racially mixed group for women offenders during a residential trip to a holiday camp:

> One evening, I attended a dance with other women in the group and we were set upon by white women holidaymakers. I was terrified, but the other black women (having always been on the receiving end of this type of behaviour) dealt with it in the most skilful way possible. It demonstrated to the white women in our group how racism worked against the black women, and reminded me as a middle class black woman how I had been protected from this in recent years since the change in my status. (Mistry, 1989, p.152)

Through experiences such as this, the group was able to move beyond developing an awareness that, as black and white working class women, group members shared similar problems which have social bases outside their immediate control and are not the result of 'individual paranoia or inadequacy' (ibid., p.150). Through the collective voice of the black women, they also confronted, for the first time, the stereotypes of black people held by their white friends.

For Foster-Carter (1987), Cashmore and Troyna (1982), and other writers (e.g. CCCS, 1982; Gilroy, 1987), the manifestation of raised black consciousness is to be found in the direct action which not only black women but others, too, have taken to minimise the pernicious impact of racism on their lives. The nature of the action has worked according to the differing circumstances in which they have found themselves. The industrial campaigns to which Foster-Carter refers(Grunwick,for example, Foster-Carter, 1987, p.50), on the surface, could not be in greater contrast to the Rastafarian movement that Cashmore and Troyna describe. However, both represent disenchantment and resistance to a mainstream society (Cashmore and Troyna,1982, p.19), which is endemically racist, and have shown the capacity to generate within specific campaigns black unity in the face of common oppression, from strikes in the work place to campaigns against police practices in the community, bringing together black young people and their parents, black men and black women, Asians and Afro Caribbeans.

The challenge to the white majority is to join the fight against racism without altering its terms. Only the black experience of oppression can give the lead. The best that can be said of white activists may be: 'They are colonised too, just like us. The only difference is we see the bars and chains' (Cashmore and Troyna, 1982, p.28). For white anti-racist advocates, the imperative is to try and understand the urgency of the struggle, and why, for black colleagues and service users, there can never be any rest from it. In this way, we can inject enhanced meaning into the statement that the personal is political, demonstrating incontrovertably that individual woes reflect social status.

A Combined Way Forward

In summary, then, there is an urgent need to fill the vacuum of empowering activity in the mainstream of professional practice, on the basis of principles of anti-oppressive working. Male as well as female workers must find a practice which supports the efforts of the women's movement (Movement for a New Society, 1983), and white practitioners, as much as black, have a responsibility to make their work actively anti-racist (Dominelli, 1988). An approach is needed which can readily be adopted by all those who share these aims and who have a genuine desire to work in a way which supports the activists' struggles. The current norm, of effectively ignoring them on the one hand or, on the other, subverting them by a failure to understand their true philosophy and impact (illustrated by any social worker who refers a woman to a refuge as if it were just another residential alternative rather than a place which actively aims to change her life) is simply not good enough at this stage in our history.

Workers who begin to talk about empowering people must be clear about what they then have the responsibility *and the skills* to deliver. Nothing would be more inexcusable than raising commitments and expectations which then flounder because the worker does not know how to deliver their contribution. Self-directed action can provide an answer because it has been developed by and with the users of mainstream welfare agencies and because, at the same time, it is rooted in anti-oppressive values. As we shall go on to illustrate in Chapter Two, the principles which underpin anti-racist, feminist, and related struggles are also embedded in self- directed work. Practitioners who use the model are challenged to combine their own efforts with those of oppressed groups without colonising them. This is achieved by placing the reins in the hands of service users organised together in groups and by offering help in achieving their own goals, in place of the customary 'we know best' of traditional practice. The detailed way this is done will be explored in Chapters Three to Six.

Groupwork: The Most Empowering and Effective Approach

Both user-led analysis and user-led action work better in groups. Consequently, self-directed action is grounded in the collective strength of people organised together.

Taking analysis first, Longres and McLeod argue that consciousness raising is best achieved within groups because it is only there that the full implications of social experiences may become apparent: 'In working with individuals and families separately, the weight is too strongly distributed in favor of individual uniqueness and private troubles' (Longres and McLeod, 1980, p.273).

As for action: in women-only groups, for example, women can 'share strategies and learn new ones from other women. They can confront and validate their right to feel as they do. They can learn of their right for space, to talk, to put across their point of view. They can formulate the kinds of services and support they need. They can see women as a support network and as a source of fun and companionship. They can overcome social isolation.

They can experience autonomy and take the initiative' (Hanmer and Statham,1988, p.132). In groups, personal troubles can be translated into common concerns. The experience of being with other people in the same boat can engender strength and new hope where apathy reigned beforehand: a sense of personal responsibility, internalised as self-blame, can find productive new outlets. Alternative explanations and new options for change and improvement can be opened up. The demoralising isolation of private misfortune reinforced by public disinterest, or even worse, moral condemnation and day-to-day surveillance, can be replaced in the course of collective enterprise with a new sense of self-confidence and potency, as well as tangible practical gains which individuals on their own could not contemplate. While none of this will be at all surprising to those who have seriously worked with groups before, it is for these reasons that it seems to us that groupwork lies at the heart of empowerment.

Groups also lend themselves to an anti-oppressive style of working. In feminist practice, for example, whilst individual work is often a necessary starting-point (Longres and McLeod, 1980, pp.273-4; Wilson, 1980, p.39; Mullender and Ward, 1985, p.171), and valuable in giving a woman 'time and space for herself' (Hanmer and Statham,1988, p.129ff), groupwork comes out on top as 'A primary method of overcoming the disparity in power between women clients and women social workers . . . . Power can be increased and shared through group participation' (ibid., p.130). The same authors observe that: 'groups can be an empowering experience for clients and social workers alike.' On the courses they ran 'women often began from a position of despair, of feeling powerless. . . . Women felt unable to effect any change, but after sharing their despair, they began to share strategies, ideas and current practice which energised everyone' (ibid., p.132).

In summary, our proposition is that groupwork can be immensely powerful if it is affiliated to a purpose which explicitly rejects the 'splintering' of the public and private, of person and society. We believe that 'to bring together clients with common needs and problems to engage in collective action on their own behalf' (Brake and Bailey, 1980, p.25) represents the essence of empowerment.

Self-Directed Groupwork

The particular groupwork model which we shall go on to describe in this book has proven to be an effective and empowering vehicle for change, based on anti-oppressive values and capable of confronting the entrenched mechanisms of power. Through resisting labels (the first practice principle we will look at in Chapter Two), raising awareness and then assisting service users in setting their own agendas for change, it has led to the achievement of apparently unattainable goals by individuals previously written off as inadequate and beyond help. This will be demonstrated in the many practice examples which will be used throughout the book.

Although not its main objective, the model leads to what we have called the 'secondary advantage' of personal change *within* the group members (Mullender and Ward, 1985, p.156) as well as to the achievement of external change. Members of these groups have appeared on national television and radio during the course of their activities, as well as addressing conferences and making presentations on professional training courses. They have grown enormously in confidence, poise and the ability to express their own views on how they see the world and their place in it.

An Accessible Model

The workers who have acted as facilitators to these groups and others like them have been ordinary field and residential social workers, teachers, community workers, youth workers, volunteers, probation officers, and Health Service professionals. They have been able to play a part in an exciting 'user revolution' because they have held firm to the practice principles which we shall explore in the next chapter. The approach they have developed to embody these values is applicable, not only with voluntary groups devoted to community action, but with any unfavourably labelled and oppressed group of people, including those for whom professionals have statutory and unavoidable responsibility.

Background to the Model

Some considerable time before the term 'empowerment' became fashionable, our involvement in developing the self-directed groupwork model marked our striving towards an understanding of the relationship between oppression, power and change. The model was rooted in groups which we went on to study but, initially, in our own practice: in the Nottingham 'Who Cares' Group, which ran a local campaign for children and young people in foster care and residential care, and in the Ainsley Teenage Action Group, a neighbourhood-based group which will be described in full in Chapter Five. (See the Appendix for a summary of all the major group examples which recur throughout this book.)

Social action groupwork with young people in trouble with the law, of which the Ainsley Group was one example, was the context both of the first full-length practice accounts (Burley, 1982; Ward, 1982b) and the earliest theoretical formulations (Ward, 1979; Ward, 1982a) of what later became self-directed groupwork. The late 1970s had seen considerable moves in the sphere of youth work towards involving young people in developing and running their own services and towards a merging of the concepts of community action and youth work (Department of Education and Science, 1969). The theory of youth work up to that time had leant heavily on social education (Davies and Gibson, 1967). Hopson and Scally (1979) introduce the term 'empowerment' but their usage encompasses only personal communication skills.

In some quarters, however, there were attempts to stretch the brief of youth work to encompass social change objectives (Davies,1979; Smith, 1980; National Youth Bureau, 1981). In Nottinghamshire at that time there were a number of linked initiatives to extend these ideas into work with young people in the social services and probation spheres (Ward, 1979 and 1982b). This sphere of operation marked the work out as separate both from youth work and from community work, though it shared its values with the radical end of the former, and its goals of community action with the latter. The practitioners involved, in looking for an appropriate term to describe their work, lighted on 'social action' as moving away from the social education roots of youth work into the 'action' of community work.

Unlike groupwork in the States, which has always had a strong social action stream within it (Coyle, 1939), practice in Britain has typically left social change goals to community workers. Indeed, it has been sharply criticised for 'de-politicising' social problems, falling to political inducement 'to see . . . new fields of practice as politically neutral - as part of the territory of professionalism' (Jordan and Parton, 1983, p.1). Once the impossibility of neutrality is recognised in that it colludes with oppression, we would argue, social action becomes inevitable. It then becomes necessary to bridge the gap between social work and community work in order to put the strategies for change used in the latter at the service of the former - and of related professional activities such as those of 'radical' health visitors working with heavily oppressed young mothers.

We knew that isolated attempts were being made to do this

because we had already started to come across individuals whose work we admired and whose values we shared. They were working to facilitate the users of mainstream services to confront oppression in its many forms and, in this way, were moving beyond analysis into action. We researched the existence of these groups (Mullender and Ward, 1988) - based on similar practice principles to our own - to see how far they extended beyond work with young people to cover all types of service user. We were looking for groups located in mainstream services which aimed to achieve external change, based on goals set by their members and which attempted to work to anti-oppressive principles. We found many initiatives beyond those involving children and young people with which we were already familiar. Other exciting developments we read about, and found examples of, included the self-advocacy movement in the fields of learning difficulties (Williams and Shoultz, 1982; Hadley, 1988; Campaign for People with Mental Handicaps, undated) and mental health (Barker and Peck, 1987; Chamberlin, 1988; Nottingham Patients Councils Support Group, 1989), the spread of organisations *of* disabled people which shared a perspective that it is social arrangements and attitudes which disable (Union of the Physically Impaired Against Segregation, 1976; Finkelstein, 1980; Nicholls et al., 1985; Derbyshire Coalition of Disabled People, 1986a and 1986b) and more isolated initiatives with other user groups, for example amongst elderly people (Flower, 1983).

Those active in these different fields typically did not recognise what they had in common with one another. Consequently, they had no occasion to meet or compare notes. Since they were all working under extreme pressure, often as an oasis of empowerment in a desert of stultifying organisational oppression, they were left to draw only on their own, rather narrowly categorised links and networks for informed support. In practice terms, as a result, they tended to have to reinvent the wheel before driving the vehicle of change. As soon as we began to conceptualise a form of intervention which was clearly taking place across all these user groups, and others, we found that we had a framework for comparison and for shared learning. We began to see the possibility of enabling the best of the innovations to traverse what were previously impervious boundaries. A generalised methodology of empowerment which had, up to this point, been so sorely lacking began to take shape.

As we gathered the practice accounts, we looked for the shape this methodology would take. We slowly began to discern in the accounts not only a shared belief in certain key values, but also a number of other constant features which had not previously been recognised as such but which, taken together, could be assembled into a clear model for practice. We tested our emerging formulation through our own continuing work, our influence as consultants and trainers, and through practice exchanges, to see whether we had expressed it fairly and clearly, and without leaving obvious gaps. This process seemed clearly to demonstrate that self-directed groupwork, as we began to call it (Mullender and Ward, 1985), was a newly-recorded approach in its own right and, furthermore, that it provided a way of moving beyond a 'common sense' approach to empowering forms of practice, by setting down a model which could be taught, transferred, debated, and refined in a constant inter-change between direct practice and theory-building.

Transferability

This formulation eventually became the self-directed groupwork model, on which this book is based. It will be set out in full in this chapter and explored in use, step by step, throughout the rest of the book. We will show how empowering practice has been and can continue to be pursued in a multiplicity of settings, with a range of user groups, and by different professional groupings. In order to assist this process of sharing and transfer, we have not used the language of social work (terms such as 'assessment' or 'intervention') but have developed a series of key phrases to summarise the basic steps in the model. These are intended to facilitate the transfer of skills and ideas between settings, disciplines and user groups since they are not peculiar to any one profession or any particular context of practice.

This is appropriate because the genesis of the model similarly bridged professional and theoretical disciplines. It was developed by social workers, community and church activists, volunteers, service users, students, community workers, youth workers, teachers, health visitors, paid and unpaid carers, and others - drawing the best from the groupwork skills and concepts, of each. They shared a grounding in certain practice principles which provided a common basis for the self-directed approach to grow. This value-base continues to allow the model to transcend the conventionally defined boundaries between the disciplines which practise groupwork. We see it as having as much to offer to teachers and adult educators, psychologists, psychiatrists and nurses, planners and architects, provided they have a 'social' or 'community' orientation to their work, as to mainstream and voluntary sector social and community workers. For all these practitioners, the approach has much to commend it. It is extremely effective in bringing about change. Furthermore, it achieves change, not with carefully selected groupings of people who are thought to be the most articulate and likely to respond but, potentially, with any groups, whether they are users of the professional services or not. The model can be adopted by a groupworker team or by a group acting on its own behalf. The latter possibility should be borne in mind at all points where, for ease of expression, the model refers to the input or views of the workers.

Having the model available means that, in future, practitioners and natural groups will have a 'ready-made' methodology of change to turn to, to help them refine their skills and techniques. This should mean that they can move ahead further and faster in their achievements. They will no longer have to trust to their instincts when, dissatisfied with the failure of traditional activity to empower service users in their particular field of practice, they depart from the tried and tested ways. We are, of course, full of praise for those workers who did take that leap of faith in the early days. (See Appendix for accounts of some of their work.) The fact that the self-directed model grew directly out of their practice is the highest testament to their achievements, and represents a valuing of the crucial contribution which thinking practitioners make to the development of more acceptable forms of intervention (Mullender and Ward, 1988). We would only add that practice, left to itself, does often fail to find time or encouragement to write about the best new ideas and, even where these are preserved, is typically not as rigorous in analysing them, as we have tried to be:

> Students and field workers alike struggle to make sense of their practice and career on a diet of ill-digested material culled from the *vox-pop* end of sociology, social policy and psychology and a host of 'practical guides' based on folk wisdom and often little else . . . . This is no accident, for it reflects both a dominant anti-intellectualism . . and a reluctance to analyse, as opposed to *record*, practise [sic]. (Jeffs and Smith, 1987, p.5)

The Model

At this point, having acknowledged the part which 'leading-edge' practitioners played in developing it, we will set out the model in the skeleton form we have devised for communicating it to others (Figure 1). There are five main stages, subdivided into twelve steps. These begin with the assembling of the worker team and the critical attention they must pay to empowering and anti-oppressive values, and take the group itself right through from starting up to evaluation.

Advantages and Disadvantages of Model-Building

We would not suggest that what actually happens in practice is

---

Figure 1. The Self-Directed Groupwork Model

Stage A: The Workers Take Stock (See Chapter Two)

This stage is essentially a pre-planning stage undertaken by the workers before making contact with users to plan the group.

Step 1: Assembling a compatible co-worker team
Step 2: Establishing appropriate consultancy support
Step 3: Agreeing on empowering principles for the work

Stage B: The Group Takes Off (See Chapter Three)

The workers next engage with users as partners to build a group, along 'open planning' lines. This initiates a style of work where users will set the norms for the group, define and analyse the problems and set the goals.

Step 4: 'Open planning'

Stage C: The Group Prepares to Take Action (See Chapter Four)

The group is helped to explore the questions WHAT?, WHY? and HOW?

Step 5: The workers facilitate the group setting its own
          agenda of issues:
          ASKING THE QUESTION - WHAT are the problems
          to be tackled?
Step 6: The workers help the group to analyse the wider
          causes of these problems:
          ASKING THE QUESTION - WHY do the
          problems exist?
Step 7: The workers enable the group to decide what action
          needs to be taken, set priorities and allocate tasks:
          ASKING THE QUESTION -HOW can we produce
          change?

---

as neatly tied and labelled as such an account may imply, nor that anyone should try to force reality to conform to the stages and steps of the model. One way of conceptualising the framework is as a grid, upon which can be placed all our ideas and actions in a piece of work, thus enabling us to see them in relation one to another, rather than in a linear progression which meanders on in an indeterminate fashion. Or, like any model, we may think of this one as a kind of map, offering practitioners some landmarks and milestones which they may recognise along the way and which they can use to get their bearings. There are many differ-

---

Stage D: The Group Takes Action (See Chapter Five)

The participants move from recognition to action:

Step 8: The participants carry out the agreed actions

Steps 5 to 8 may recur, perhaps several times, before the group moves on. As they raise participants' confidence, they become self-reinforcing.

Stage E: The Group Takes Over (See Chapter Six)

The group goes on to see the connections between WHAT, WHY and HOW. In other words, participants extend their attention to broader issues and wider-scale campaigning. Meanwhile, the workers move increasingly into the background and may leave the group altogether. As well as 'taking over' the running of their group, participants are, by this stage, learning to take control of their own lives and of the way others perceive them. Their much improved self-esteem tells them that they have a right to do this.

Step 9: The group reviews what it has achieved.
Step 10: The group identifies new issues to be tackled
        - REFORMULATING WHAT?
Step 11: The group perceives the links between the different
        issues tackled
        - REFORMULATING WHY?
Step 12: The group decides what actions to take next
        - REFORMULATING HOW?

Steps (9) to (12) become a continuing process throughout the group's life.

ent paths to the goal which, to some extent, pass by these markers in varying orders - some of them many times! There are a few rules, however. We know from experience, for example, that workers who do not carry out their pre-planning rigorously will find themselves back at 'Go' before very long, and looking for a better route!

Presenting the model in this form does have other advantages besides transferability, as Henderson and Thomas (1980, Chapter One) suggest. Firstly, once the workers have established a basic sense of direction (in our case by working out their practice principles in the pre-planning stage) they will be able 'to disaggregate . . . the work into workable and meaningful steps, in each of which there are a variety of tasks to be carried out'. Secondly, there will be phases of reflection and re-planning during which they - together with group members - can stand back to review progress and think through the likely consequences of alternative courses of action. This can safeguard against 'unthinking activism'; that is, taking on more commitments than workers or participants can handle (ibid., p.26)

Just as the model has been tested and modified since we first formulated it, it will need to go on being refined in the light of experience. It is neither perfected nor static, but must stand or fall on whether it is viable in practice with the capacity to encompass valid new practical and critical challenges as these present themselves.

We shall now go on in the next five chapters to give a full exposition of the model, organised within the five-stage basic framework. The 'key phrases' from the model, which we have used to name and differentiate the stages and steps, will reappear as a framework for the ensuing chapters. Thus, in Chapter Two we begin with the workers 'Taking Stock', particularly of the value-base of the approach, as they come together to use the model. In Chapters Three to Six - as the group 'Takes Off', 'Prepares to Take Action' (through asking the questions WHAT, WHY and HOW), puts that action into effect and, finally, increasingly 'Takes Over'. We will look in detail at the activities and major practice issues which are typical of each of these subsequent stages of the approach, illustrated throughout by a range of practice examples. The importance of values in marking out the distinctive nature of each stage of the approach will be highlighted throughout. Informed by these, self-directed action, together with the knowledge and experience users gain from carrying it out, forms an essential platform for a systematic, structurally grounded challenge to the degrading and stigmatising conditions which are the practical manifestation of oppression. On this basis, users and workers can begin to chip away at all the forms of inequality that lie at the heart of current oppressive social arrangements.

Chapter Two

The Workers Take Stock:
The Centrality of Values

In Chapter One, we presented the history and the bare framework of self-directed groupwork, stressing the crucial role within it - if practice is to be both empowering and effective - of clear and appropriate values aimed at anti-oppressive working. In this chapter, we will explore these underpinning values in greater detail, showing that they constitute most of the 'meat' of Stage A of the model, once the worker team has assembled and established its support mechanisms. We will then go on to illustrate in later chapters how the values lead naturally into the key features of the model, such as the open style of planning which fully involves service users (Chapter Three) and their full participation in setting the goals for, carrying out, and evaluating action aimed at achieving the changes they see as essential (Chapters Four to Six). Overall, in this and the following four chapters, we shall be offering a complete and value-based methodology for empowering practice.

Getting Our Own Act Together

To start with the values, then, we believe that we owe it to service users to clarify where we stand before making spoken or unspoken claims upon their time, their trust in us, or their flagging hope that the circumstances causing them distress and indignity may be susceptible to change.

It is not uncommon for workers to expect to swing into action clad in nothing more than anti-authoritarian zeal and a loose commitment to tackling oppression. It is not good enough to have no cogent responses ready when users throw out remarks like: 'We've been written off now. Nobody listens to us. What can the likes of us do? Who can we complain to? We'll just have to learn to live with it.' These are not direct quotes, but typically accusing and fatalistic sentiments which we believe workers need to think about *before* they offer their services to users rather than after.

These issues need to be tackled in this first stage of the model as an essential precursor to asking users to engage with us in any process of work aimed at change. It is insulting and patronising to have no response to their perfectly realistic doubts, and yet to invite - or even expect - their co-operation. For the most vulnerable, who have known only repressive and institutionalising services but who have at least found their own survival mechanisms within that deadening context, it is insulting to upset that stasis if we have only rhetoric to offer in its place. For the more hard-bitten service users, who have heard and seen it all before and who are tired of workers rushing in, promising the earth, failing, and retreating to the comfort of their own lives, it is patronising to expect a suspension of disbelief in your methods and abilities unless you offer positive proof by making the work user-led right from the start. This is why we place such emphasis on involving users in basic planning, as will be seen in Chapter Three.

Stage A of the Model: Pre-Planning

Before the workers even meet with service users, then, we have found it essential that they themselves should go through a kind of 'pre-planning stage'. The tasks to be accomplished during this are, firstly, to come together as a worker team; secondly, if at all possible, to find the backing of a skilled consultant; and, thirdly, and most importantly, to agree on their fundamental values, that is, the principles underlying their work.

Step 1. *Assembling a Compatible Co-Worker Team*

Deciding whether to work alone or with others and, if the latter, establishing an effective and skilled co-working relationship is the first step in this pre-planning. Self-directed groups normally have at least two workers who support each other in attempting to put their values into operation. The ability to co-work effectively, often across professional boundaries, is therefore a fundamental skill in self-directed groupwork. Such collaboration requires, for example, well-developed communication skills directed to the tasks in hand, full recording of planning and, later, of group process, adequate back-up from a consultant, and the ability to channel the lessons both from what is recorded and from the professional support mechanisms back into the planning and the groupwork itself.

ADVANTAGES OF CO-WORKING

Most of the advantages of co-working are shared with other forms of groupwork, but there are some differences of emphasis in self-directed work. A general listing of the advantages of co-working is provided by Hodge (1985, pp.2-3). Apart from the fact that he uses the concept of 'leadership', whereas we shall explain later in this chapter why we prefer 'facilitation', the only point in Hodge's list which would not apply here is that of being able to share the impact of the dependency of participants on the workers. We would not see dependency as appropriate in self-directed action. In all other respects, we would agree with him that co-working is helpful to the group because it is an enriching experience, with a greater degree of attentiveness to members' contributions and feelings, and a broader range of role modelling available, including that of positive interaction between the workers. We are also in broad accord with Brown (1986, pp.58-59) who further itemises the kind of richness that two workers can offer to a group - from balanced racial or gender pairings, to contrasted personal styles, knowledge or skills. Page (1983, p.11), writing from the perspective of a community worker, shows that it is not just in therapeutic groupwork that members benefit from the opportunity to find they relate better to one or the other of the workers' personalities, and that new initiatives may arise more freely where relationships do not become too 'cosy'.

Beyond benefits to participants, Hodge draws out the assistance that co-working offers to the workers themselves. They can receive mutual support, feedback, and back up: both practical, when roles need to be shared or one person is unable to attend, and emotional, when a second view is needed, or one worker feels deskilled or is less experienced than the other (Hodge, 1985, pp.2-3). To this, Brown adds the possibility of mutual professional development, the pooling of administrative tasks and simple worker preference (Brown, 1986, pp.59-60). His other stated advantage, of sharing actively controlling functions within groups which require them, is one which actually would not apply in self-directed work, where group consensus must be reached.

We would add to these lists a further crucial benefit of shared practice: that is, that co-workers can assist one another in holding to anti-oppressive ways of working. Given that oppression as an issue has been shown to lie at the core of empowerment (see Chapter One), co-working has an important part to play in assisting work to take due account of its impact on users, and in avoiding the replication of oppressive structures and relationships. Published accounts of projects (Badham, 1989, p. 29 and p.31; Mistry 1989, pp.153-4) have stressed the importance of co-workers jointly developing coherent practice which incorporates a black perspective, for example. Mistry describes how, in the mixed race women's group run by herself and a white co-worker, they shared common experiences as women, but 'as a black woman I had the specific experience of racism which could be shared with other black group members' (ibid., p.153). She and her co-worker worked hard to build on their shared commitment to, but different perspectives on, feminism in the context of a strong co-working partnership.

Moving on to the decision whether to have two or more co-workers, Stock Whitaker (1975, p.437) is against the latter: 'A good rule to follow is not to include more than two staff'. We are of the opinion, however, that larger groups may need more workers - we would certainly not see two workers as necessarily ideal with a group of forty or more members (see the section in the next chapter on group size). There is a need for workers in self-directed groups to be attentive to group process at a level of concentration which two workers would find it hard to maintain, in order to ensure that the process remains empowering for all.

Step 2. *Establishing Appropriate Consultancy Support*

In addition to deciding whether to work in conjunction with others, those initiating self-directed work have to decide whether to work with a consultant and, if so, who this should be. The isolated workers from whose practice the self-directed model first developed, did not always have the advantage of consultancy support (or, arguably worse, were sometimes working with someone who did not understand their aims and principles) and yet, clearly, they made great strides in challenging accepted norms and pioneering a new approach. It would be precious of us, therefore, to suggest that work not underpinned by appropriate consultancy is more likely to fail. What we *would* say is that it may be more frustrating and more subject to dead-ends and false starts. As Keenan and Pinkerton (1988, p.237) put it: 'workers need to include in their support network at least one contact which gets them out of the quagmire of personal introspection, group process, and agency pressure, so as to work on clarifying and modifying their sense of direction; their personal practice ideology'.

Like Brown (1986, p.61) and Hodge (1985, pp.6-8 and p.15), then, we would regard the availability of skilled supervision and consultancy, if this can possibly be managed - as well as adequate time before and between group meetings to use it - as the best means of resolving any possible problems. As will be shown in the next section, it is essential that, with or without a consultant present, this time be used in the early stages to establish an agreed value position. However, we would have additional reasons for stressing the advantages of supported feedback and planning at this early stage:

a. a consultant can challenge the workers to formulate and clarify their agreed value position around anti-oppressive aims;
b. a consultant can challenge the workers to hold to their value position when later planning or the work itself begins to deviate from the agreed principles under the pressure of day-to-day realities, or when different workers favour different solutions to a practical dilemma;
c. the model of intervention is a relatively new one - it may not yet be fully absorbed into workers' basic assumptions about practice so it can be useful to have someone continually drawing their attention back to the fundamental principles they have agreed on, such as throwing decisions back to group members, thus avoiding the tendency to slip back into old ways of working;
d. both the skills and the techniques can feel new and unfamiliar - they may need discussing and rehearsing in privacy and safety, with an impartial observer, before being used in practice;
e. the development of self-directed groups is far less predictable than many other forms of groups - someone experienced in using the model can provide reassurance and meeting them regularly offers the space in which to examine what is happening over time;
f. in order to be effective facilitators in a group, workers need to be very clear about their own respective roles and to establish an open style of communication between themselves - a consultant can help them to maintain this when the going gets rough;
g. a consultant can have an important role in avoiding the dangers of co-working (Hodge, 1985, pp. 4-5), notably disagreements between the workers about the group or about agendas brought in from outside it;
h. any new or unfamiliar form of practice is bound to lead to a certain amount of suspicion, or even opposition, from those

outside the immediate worker team; a consultant can help them to be ready to answer their critics and to trust one another to respond appropriately at times when there is no chance to prepare a collective strategy or reply.

Over all, then, the consultant can encourage the workers to plan for, and later to discuss, group process and worker style based on empowering values. This helps them to be efficient enablers to the group and not to hinder it by slipping back into more conventional ways of planning or working, or by being unaware of the direction in which things are moving, or by failing to keep open communication amongst themselves or with group members.

The consultant's own style of operation should also, of course, be consistent with the values we will be discussing later in this chapter (Keenan and Pinkerton, 1988, p.229). They must hear and value what the workers bring to their role, enable them to 'own' the decisions they make about the group and push them to consider structural factors which underlie members' circumstances, for example. The person who plays this role ideally needs to have had personal experience of self-directed practice, therefore. This is valuable, not only in helping them to follow and channel the flow of discussion, but also because their interventions should set an appropriate tone for the resulting practice. Indeed, the consultant often directly models the worker role. This is done, for example, by facilitating rather than leading discussion and by using classic self-directed techniques like brainstorming and prioritising exercises (see Chapter Four for an outline of these), notably when the workers are planning for the group. Later, as well as helping the practitioners to focus on key issues, the consultant may be able to use these techniques to draw any unacknowledged conflict out into the open before handing it back to the workers themselves to resolve - just as they will need to do in the group.

Step 3. *Agreeing on Empowering Principles for the Work*

As was established in Chapter One, the self-directed model rests on an explicit statement of values which has clear implications for practice. Indeed, these values are firmly enmeshed in self-directed action; they cannot be verbally acknowledged but then ignored when it really counts - in the work itself. Conventional groupwork tends to be preoccupied with getting straight into the process of starting a group, taking values for granted. The first stage of the self-directed model, on the other hand, involves the workers in thrashing out their shared value position before they engage in what would more normally be the first stage: that of preparing to initiate a piece of practice. This can be a protracted and perhaps acerbic process. At least one full meeting, and perhaps several, is likely to be required in order for each individual to state where they stand before similarities and differences of view become clear.

Only preliminary consensus about the sources from which ideology and understanding flow can assure the success of the resultant intervention. It may well be that agreement cannot, in fact, be arrived at and that either the plans are aborted at this early stage, or that one person withdraws their involvement. This is vastly preferable, however, to ploughing on regardless. Submerged or unrecognised differences will always emerge at some later point, usually at a time of the utmost sensitivity, to haunt the practitioners and quite probably cause unnecessary distress to service users.

An example from practice illustrates what happens when a worker team leaves conflict unexpressed and hence fails to reach an agreed value position. The members of the Rowland Dale Group (a disguised name; see also Rogowski and McGrath, 1986, and Mullender, 1989/90) were parents who had physically abused their children. Two out of the three group- workers saw structural inequalities as the root cause of the abuse, whilst the third blamed individual personal inadequacy. She could not accept that more money or better housing would help because, in her view, the families concerned would not know what to do with these and would end up in difficulties all over again. She left the group after only a few meetings, during which the workers had tended too often to be preoccupied with their own differences of opinion and sometimes distracted from drawing out the views and experiences of members. This happened, in large part, because the workers' conflicting views were not acknowledged or dealt with before the group commenced and there was no consultant to help draw them out. This could have eased the path for the third worker to have opted out before the group started, rather than after.

A Statement of Values: Principles for Empowering Practice

Now we turn to the values themselves. We hold strongly to the view that there is no such thing as value-free or value-neutral work (Bernstein, 1972, p.155); there are only workers who have not stopped to think what their values actually are. Unless workers define and explore their own values before beginning groupwork, the group is less likely to succeed because 'the enterprise is flying blind' (ibid., p.145).

Even when practitioners assume that their work *is* informed by values, their thinking is often wishy-washy and based on vague concepts, which apparently no one could disagree with, such as 'respect for persons'. (See Timms, 1983 and elsewhere, and Shardlow, 1989, for fuller discussions of the problematic nature of 'values' in social work.) Disagreement with the traditional values of social work has, though, begun to be voiced. Hudson (1985, p.640) incisively points out that the sensitivity to human needs which such terms appear to claim can 'act as a mask to blind us to the quite subtle and diffuse ways that social work replicates dominant meanings about femininity and masculinity and how social workers often collude with the complex pattern of subordination of women in our society'. Dominelli (1989, p.12) writes in similar vein:

> Social workers' traditional image of themselves as tolerant professionals improving the quality of life for clients by according them dignity and self-worth ... has recently been questioned by academicians, practitioners and clients. Particularly devastating critiques of current practice have been mounted by black people and feminists who have pronounced social work as oppressive, reinforcing racism, sexism, and social control.

It is safer, then, to judge workers from what they actually do than from what they claim are their values. A truly empowering approach is observable from its impact on service users.

Five Practice Principles

1. We need to take a view of the people we work with which refuses to accept negative labels and recognises instead that *all people have skills, understanding and ability* .
2. People have rights, including *the right to be heard* and the right to control their own lives. It follows that people also have the right to choose what kinds of intervention to accept in their

lives. *Service users must always be given the right to decide whether or not to participate in self-directed work, and the right to define issues and take action on them* .

3. The problems that service users face are complex and responses to them need to reflect this. People's problems can never be fully understood if they are seen solely as a result of personal inadequacies. Issues of oppression, social policy, the environment and the economy are, more often than not, and particularly in the lives of service users, major contributory forces. *Practice should reflect this understanding* .

4. *Practice can effectively be built on the knowledge that people acting collectively can be powerful.* People who lack power can gain it through working together in groups.

5. *Practise what you preach.* Methods of working must reflect non-elitist principles:

a. workers do not 'lead' the group but facilitate members in making decisions for themselves and in controlling whatever outcome ensues. Though special skills and knowledge are employed, these do not accord privilege and are not solely the province of the workers;

b. all our work must *challenge oppression* whether by reason of race, gender, sexual orientation, age, class, disability, or any other form of social differentiation upon which spurious notions of superiority and inferiority have historically been (and continue to be) built and kept in place by the exercise of power.

These essential principles will now be explored in greater detail.

Principle 1:

We need to take a view of the people we work with which refuses to accept negative labels and recognises instead that *all people have skills, understanding and ability* .

REFUSING TO ACCEPT NEGATIVE LABELS

The people we work with cannot be dismissed as 'mad' or 'bad'. Nor can they be defined, or encapsulated by depersonalising terms such as 'delinquents', 'the handicapped', 'the elderly', 'inadequate mothers', and so on. One of the greatest dangers with such labels is that one disabling characteristic, or one incident of behaviour accounted as unacceptable, can be enough to suck an individual into a system of treatment, containment or punishment, after which their whole functioning may be called into question and all opportunity to control their own lives removed.

To use a phrase adopted in the field of learning difficulties, we have to re-learn to see service users as 'people first'. That is, they are ordinary people who are facing distressing and oppressing difficulties/difficult circumstances in their lives, sometimes at the hands of the welfare services themselves, which would leave anyone who is less than superhuman struggling to cope. They are probably also facing adverse attitudes and prejudice against them, and there can be a tendency for them to absorb these attitudes themselves and to come to believe that they are justified. This is the phenomenon of oppressed people taking on the values of the oppressor which is very familiar, for example, to feminists confronting unaware women who say they feel flattered by wolf whistles, or safer if they rely on a man.

'Refusing to accept' negative labels may be an understatement of the effort which can be involved, both for the service users, who can find themselves at every turn defined on the basis of the dismissive definition, and for the worker, who may be shaking off the habits of an entire career. Colleagues, or a whole working ethos, may also need to be confronted - as in challenging the sick humour of social work offices, excused as a survival mechanism but insidious in its permeation of practitioners' attitudes and its de-personalising of group members. Language can also patronise through being incomprehensible, or through mystification - as if workers were party to some grand field of knowledge way over group members' head. In fact, words which stem directly from group members' own experiences will always tend to be more powerful, for example in the images they convey to people outside the group, as well as more empowering for members themselves in that they ground the group in members' own reality and validate their own perceptions. Generally, group members are much better at 'cutting through the crap' of labelling and professional mystification.

VALUING THE STRENGTHS IN PEOPLE

We consider that not only do those we work with not deserve the negative labels which are pinned on them but, in fact, they are full of positives: they have strengths, skills, understanding, the ability to do things for themselves, and much to offer one another. Laming and Sturton (1978, p.121), in their widescale introduction of groupwork to a particular local authority, reported this latter point as being especially valued by service users. These qualities are frequently underestimated, overlooked or disbelieved by other people who fail to look beyond the negative labels people have derived from their previous contacts with the authorities which exist to police or ameliorate their lives. Once people are accorded basic respect, however, they can begin to shine as very much more sharp and able than had ever been assumed by anyone, including themselves.

This is the true revelation of empowering practice - just how strong, capable and aware service users are, and what they can achieve for themselves. It is like going through the looking glass and finding that a world of quite different possiblities opens up on the other side. 'Humans are naturally powerful. The manifestations of powerlessness are only the social teachings we have digested' (Pike, undated, p.16).

Users can and do break out of the mould, either through their own efforts alone, or through a reversal of the self-fulfilling prophecy to which workers have previously subscribed (Smale, 1977). If service users are treated as the problem ('This job would be easy if it weren't for the clients') and as stupid, then they will be so, because they will be perceived as so and because they will sometimes live up to the perception in order to fit in with what is expected of them. If, on the other hand, they are asked to contribute their ideas, are really listened to, and then are encouraged to act on their own suggestions, those same people will present very differently. Teenage mothers attending a group run by health visitors and a social work student and initially assuming that they would be asked to discuss problems in coping with their babies, were enabled to show, instead, that they already knew most of the stuff about caring for children but could not put it into effect because of lack of money, inadequate housing and the constant drain on energy and their own health posed by battering partners. They brought out extremely perceptive views of male/female relationships and of the status of women in contemporary society and gave evidence of their own remarkable resilience as sheer survivors in the face of sexual abuse, neglect and physical ill-treatment in their own childhood.

Principle 2:

People have rights, including the right to be heard and the right to control their own lives. It follows that people also have the right to choose what kinds of intervention to accept in their lives. *Service users must always be given the right to decide whether or not to participate in self-directed work, and the right to define issues and take action on them* .

THE RIGHT TO CHOOSE

Once people's strengths and abilities are recognised, the practice which flows from this recognition has to accord people a far greater role in choosing what kinds of intervention they will accept in their lives and whether to get involved in directing their own process of change. Choices can only be made on the basis of full information about the alternatives. It is no longer tenable for workers to deprive users of key information about the options on the assumption that they 'know best'. People must be let into the professional 'secrets' about possible types of intervention and where the resources come from which make them possible; they must be empowered to opt into or out of groups and campaigns, to define their own issues, and to set their own agenda for change.

THE RIGHT TO BE HEARD

The first step in any programme of change is for groups of service users to find their own voice. Typically, they have never been listened to before. This valuing of their views helps service users to find the words to express opinions and experiences which have hitherto remained keenly felt but unaired. For workers who are new to this way of working, it can come as a shock to hear how trenchant and strongly felt are the results. The experience of being part of collective efforts towards change makes those who participate in it more articulate, more confident, and more aware. We have called this the 'secondary advantage' of personal change within service users because it is not the primary purpose for which self-directed action is undertaken (Mullender and Ward, 1985, p.156).

Once service users begin to find a voice, there are three separate areas on which the workers need to encourage them to express their opinions. (The ways in which this can be done will be looked at in more detail in Chapter Four.) Firstly, there is the question of their own perception of the problems which confront them. That is straightforward enough, although it remains relatively unusual for workers to act on an assessment by service users of what is wrong, rather than on their own. Normally, being labelled as a client puts this out of the question (Breakwell, 1989, p.14).

The next step is still more crucial. In self-directed work, it is not sufficient for group members merely to be helped to articulate 'WHAT' they experience as their most troublesome problems and then to move directly to 'HOW' they propose to tackle them. It is a central tenet of the ideology behind the model that, as an intervening step, they should also be facilitated in elucidating the reasons 'WHY' these problems have come to exist. Only then will they arrive at the most appropriate ways of tackling them.

Taking a group of teenagers in trouble with the law as an example, they might consider that 'WHAT' is the matter is the fact that the police have been paying them too much attention. They are continually told, from all sides, that 'HOW' to stop this happening is for them to behave themselves, stay at home and not draw themselves to police attention. Yet this entirely leaves out of account the role of the police themselves in the continual confrontations of which the young people complain. It colludes with the view that these are always the youngsters' own fault. It is only when the question 'WHY?' is asked - in this case 'WHY' do the police pick on particular young people? - that we open up the broad and crucial issues of the role, conduct and control of policing in our society, its failure to be even-handed with the different social classes, age groups and racial groupings within our cities, and general attitudes towards young men on council estates.

Many further, graphic examples could be given. The Rowland Dale Group (mentioned earlier), for example, consisted of parents who had physically abused their children. They were frequently accused of individual failure to cope, and individually subjected to the full weight of a child abuse system which still, at the time of writing, gives very little information to parents about what is happening or what their own legal rights may be. Yet, through talking to one another in the group, they realised that they shared the perspective that 'WHY' they had been driven to hitting their children was because of the tremendous pressures placed on them by inadequate incomes and housing. To this, the inquisitorial and judgemental style of many social workers and health visitors simply added yet more pressure. A further realisation was that, once they had acknowledged their own view of 'WHY' the abuse happened, *and that they all shared its effects*, they could move on beyond feeling that that was how life was - extremely unfair but there was nothing one could do about it. In fact, there was a great deal that could be done about it *together*, such as learning their rights in the benefits and housing fields, challenging the authorities to change their rules or exercise them more fairly, and beginning to campaign on a national level for governmental action on poverty. Without the consideration of 'WHAT', 'WHY' and 'HOW' in that order (but often repeated many times), there can be no awakening awareness either of wider-scale oppression or of the possibility of moving beyond fatalism and self-pity into raised consciousness and the pursuit of rights.

CONTROL OVER THE AGENDA OF ACTION

Group members are fully involved in determining the purpose and goals of the self-directed group (the 'HOW?' of intervention) through completely shared decision making. Much has been written elsewhere about the nature of true participation (Arnstein, 1969; Stiefel and Pearse, 1982; Richardson, 1983; Hallett, 1987; Wilson, V., 1988), and we will not repeat it here. Suffice it to say that the self-directed model is a non-starter unless control of the group's aims and objectives is handed over to its members. Only the members' perspective on selecting and defining those problems which are of central concern in their lives can move the group onto a different plane from worker-inspired and worker-led groupwork, by engaging them completely as part of the process and not just as the passive recipients of the change efforts which are made in the group.

What is more, only the knowledge that they really are at the helm will engender in the participants the kinds of personal change, referred to above as a secondary advantage of this form of work, through channelling their energy and vision towards realisable goals.

Principle 3:

The problems that service users face are complex and responses to them need to reflect this. People's problems can never be fully understood if they are seen solely as a result of personal inadequacies. Issues of oppression, social policy, the environment and the economy are, more often than not, and particularly in the lives of service users, major contributory forces. *Practice should reflect this understanding* .

COMPLEX PROBLEMS AND EXTERNAL CHANGE

Once service users' negative labels begin to be challenged, and once their own views on the circumstances they face begin to be sought, a far more complex range of factors must be taken into account. Typically, social workers are daunted by this kind of analysis because they do not see how they can incorporate it into their own everyday practice. Self-directed action empowers practitioners to bridge this gap just as much as it empowers service users.

The view that macro social problems can begin to be resolved through campaigning at a micro, that is a localised or personal level, opens up many doors which have appeared shut for practitioners in the past. Typically, an unbridgeable gap has been assumed to exist between what the individual worker can set in train on the one hand (other than through political or trade union activity - both normally conceived of as lying outside the individual's actual work responsibilities and in some other realm of duties as a concerned citizen), and, on the other, the sort of changes which would require government instigation.

Parton, for example, in considering what more can be done to prevent the physical abuse and neglect of children, regards the only route to a solution as 'a realignment in social policy' (Parton, 1985, p.176). The aim of this would be to 'reduce the general levels of poverty, stress, insecurity, ill-health and bad housing' (ibid., p.187). We do not disagree that social policy decisions have made matters far worse, or that 'the first priority must be a comprehensive anti-poverty strategy' (ibid., p.188). Nevertheless, whereas Parton sees this only in the context of central governmental priorities, our work has shown the potential for action which begins at a local level to move beyond parochial issues into campaigning for change at a national level. This process can be seen at work wherever the establishment of a small, local group has led to the burgeoning of other such groups elsewhere and, eventually, to the creation of a national body which can take up the campaigning on a wider scale - such as NAYPIC (The National Association of Young People in Care), for example. Through the use of self-directed groupwork, workers can do far more, in our opinion, than just tell people what their rights are (Parton, ibid., pp.193-198).

Principle 4:

Practice can effectively be built on the knowledge that people acting collectively can be powerful. People who lack power can gain it through working together in groups.

COLLECTIVE POWER

What we do, then, is to draw people together into groups to 'empower' them to tackle problems external to themselves, normally on a localised basis at first, but often broadening out to attain national dimensions when tackled in conjunction with others. Through them, often the wider communities of interest which they represent are also empowered. We have, in Chapter One, already argued the importance and potential of groups in working for change and will not repeat this here.

This process means that intervention is directed explicitly at helping those who are relatively powerless to become more powerful. For this to be possible, it is necessary for the worker to be willing really to *hear* when service users say that structural problems are uppermost in their lives and, crucially, to make the leap of faith to see these as approachable through the medium of user-directed action.

Principle 5:

Practise what you preach. Methods of working must reflect non-elitist principles:

a) workers do not 'lead' the group but facilitate members in making decisions for themselves and in controlling whatever outcome ensues. Though special skills and knowledge are employed, these do not accord privilege and are not solely the province of the workers;

b) all our work must *challenge oppression* whether by reason of race, gender, sexual orientation, age, class, disability, or any other form of social differentiation upon which spurious notions of superiority and inferiority have historically been (and continue to be) built and kept in place by the exercise of power.

A) WORKERS AS FACILITATORS

Workers must want to work with people and not to direct intervention to or at them. The groupworker must consequently regard his or her most effective contribution as being facilitation rather than leadership in the traditional sense, which has quite different *power* connotations. It is always essential to question to what ends the worker's control is directed, and over which areas of the group's functioning it is exercised and to look out for retreats into old-style leadership assumptions. The worker may betray a misplaced sense of professional 'ownership' of the group through the use of terminology such as 'my group', for example. Power is never value-free or value-neutral as Douglas (1976, pp.71-73) appears to imply when he treats both the degree and the sources of the groupworker's power as questions primarily of control - of what makes the worker most effective. In our view power is, by definition, 'value-laden' (Lukes, 1974, p.57). Leadership can never be simply a technical exercise in management; it necessarily stems from explicit or implicit intentions and purposes. Empowerment relies on asking who determines those intentions and purposes and handing back the power over decision-making to service users.

The role that the workers expect to play will require particularly careful elucidation with members because it will be an unfamiliar one to many people. More common experiences in groups, from school onwards, tend to be of being instructed what to do. It needs to be clear from the start, therefore, that workers whose intention is to empower will be placing full responsibility on members to decide what action to take.

Special Skills and Knowledge
Workers assist with finding means to achieve the group's desired ends, then, but they do not dictate what those ends should be. They may well make suggestions and offer alternative scenarios for consideration by group members but their chief involvement will be in easing and highlighting group process, not in influencing the direction of the work undertaken by the group or its outcome.

This style of working is essential if the earlier principles are to be observed. Opening themselves up to hearing what service users are saying (Principle 2), empowering them to set their own goals (Principle 3) and taking collective action (Principle 4), implies drawing out the best from group members and helping them to determine where they want the group to go, rather than imposing one's own agendas onto them. Workers can, however, have a hard job explaining and maintaining this in the group. Members are more used to professionals as authority figures, and as providers or with-holders of resources. Consequently, they will expect the workers to tell them what to do and how to do it, and to procure everything the group needs to make it function. It takes frequent direct explanation and practical demonstrations for group members to recognise that they can look to the workers for help but not for instruction. Workers have initially to be directive about being non-directive.

Often, people who are unfamiliar with the role fall into the trap of going too far the other way and becoming totally non-interventive. This is not what is implied by facilitation. It does not mean falling over backwards to keep one's self and one's own views invisible and unheard. It means playing an active role - for example, in challenging the fatalism which members often bring to a new group: 'But there's nothing we can do about it' - yet being sensitive to the differences between keeping issues in play and dominating.

In view of the subtle judgements that are involved, there is certainly no less skill involved in this kind of work than in groupwork which is led from the centre. There are specific methods and techniques which help to empower service users and these can be studied, learned, practised and evaluated. This will be apparent in the chapters which follow, when we explore what workers actually do. Groups can require facilitation at any or all stages of the process: in coming together to share their experiences, in finding the means to form views and set goals, and in generating the knowledge and skills needed to carry out tasks.

All this means that empowerment practice is a skilled discipline. We would argue that, even within voluntary groups (whether or not they have paid workers), the role of facilitator needs to be played and that groups could sometimes make better progress by acknowledging this need within their own internal organisation. Office holders or key members within self-directed groups can often play the role very well, but may appreciate the same consultancy and other support as paid workers. We would suggest that parts of this book could be as useful to them as to professional workers, though no doubt they already hold to clear value positions within their respective organisations.

Where, in contrast, workers are paid to perform the facilitator's role, they must be prepared to demonstrate their responsibility for themselves and to the group. It is not sufficient merely to claim goodwill, commitment or an idealised notion of equality (Barker, 1986; Keenan and Pinkerton, 1988, pp.233-237). Members have a right to expect skilled help (Barker, ibid., p.86) and effective structures for evaluation by users. We will consider this in greater detail in Chapter Six, but would say at this stage that work on putting these structures in place actually needs to start at the beginning of a group, not the end.

Not only are self-directed groupworkers active and skilful, but they also have rights of their own within the group. Sometimes, new workers get hold of the idea that, because workers in self-directed groups do not impose agendas on the members, they therefore must express no views and set no boundaries of their own. In fact, since involvement is constructed as a partnership of workers and users, it would be dishonest for workers not to share the things they feel strongly about. It would also be misleading because expectations and assumptions are taken for granted as being in agreement with the group, if left unspoken.

It is essential to be honest with members about your 'bottom line' , about what you can and cannot accept. It is perfectly appropriate, for example, for the groupworkers to say at the outset that they retain a veto on their continued involvement with the group. This can be used if the members decide after full consideration to pursue an objective with which the workers refuse to be identified - such as trying to get the blacks off their estate - and if attempts at challenging this and opening up further discussion all fail. As it would not be acceptable to stay involved under these circumstances, the workers would have to say that they could not go along with the proposed actions and leave the group.

Facilitation Not Solely the Province of Workers

Facilitation functions are not the special province of workers. Group maintenance, for example, is shared as far as possible with group members, and increasingly so over time. The group itself needs to learn the skills of 'resolving interpersonal conflict' (Brown, 1986, p.54) but also to recognise that such expressions of hostility, as of self-blame, can represent a misdirecting of anger which could more fruitfully be focused on the actual source of their oppression, and hence channelled into energy to achieve external change. Where a worker does exercise such functions, it is important to remember that this is done, not through any special privilege or superior understanding, but on behalf of the group.

Group maintenance functions have to be adapted to the value framework of empowerment and exercised in a style which is compatible with its overall principles. 'Expressing group feelings' (Douglas, 1976, p.71) or 'evaluating the emotional climate' (Brown, 1986, p.54) - to give a further example of the worker holding no specially privileged power - requires that the worker should merely state what he or she is experiencing, not attempt to interpret it. Where a worker does try to pick up and voice the prevailing mood or feelings in the group (which can assist participants' voices to be heard, according to Principle 2), members must at all times feel perfectly free to disagree with what the worker has sensed to be the case - there should be no hierarchy of control over this, just as there is not over any other aspect of the group's functioning, or the group cannot be empowering.

Though we adapt them, we do not undervalue group maintenance functions. Page (1983, pp.9-10) highlights the reality of social action as requiring the skills to deal with people who have little or no experience of working collectively and who may need a good deal of individual support within the group early on, mediating conflict, and attempting to mend relationships where trust has broken down. As a feminist, Page argues that these personal, or process, aspects of work must be recognised and attended to as carefully as the macho-sounding issues of strategies, campaigns, tactics and action. If we are serious about Principle 5, we have to rethink the meta-language which we use to talk about 'acting' as much as the action itself, since the two are heavily intertwined.

B) An Anti-Oppressive Style of Work

In all our work, in order to be consistent with the principles already listed above, we have to be determined to challenge oppression - whether by reason of race, gender, sexual orientation, age, class, or disability. We need to recognise that this requires continual efforts to confront prejudice in ourselves as well as in others.

Race

Worker teams need to be committed to developing effective anti-racist practice. Some of the most empowering work has been developed by black workers specifically with black people: examples have included an Asian girls' group, focusing on what it feels like to be growing up black in a white society and how the members might take more control over their own lives in ways which would not alienate them from their own families; and a black youth and community centre, run and managed by its users and incorporating voluntary work activities, social events, a pool room, a group run on behalf of the local statutory agencies with young people who refused to engage with social workers and probation officers, advice on setting up small businesses, information on job vacancies, and much else besides. There is an urgent need to develop many more projects like these.

Opening up opportunities for black workers to undertake work with black service users is only one aspect of anti-racist practice, however. Mixed worker teams must also enable black and white people to work together through drawing on common concerns and interests, as has been done with young people in the inner city of Nottingham in helping them to organise an annual Rock and Reggae Festival for over ten years. Here, a voluntary sector youth work agency, Nottingham Young Volunteers, working to empower local resident volunteers, encouraged them to plan and organise a festival of black and white music performed and enjoyed by the youth of the area in their thousands. Recently, it has expanded to encompass Asian Bhangra music as well as a whole host of other arts, dance, poetry and drama events, children's play activities and stalls. The principles on which the work was based included a commitment to ensuring that organisers and performers reflected the make up of the local community, that the organisation and the event itself should 'actively challenge divisions based on race or sex or class within the context of presenting an event which is accessible and enjoyable for all' (Social Action Training, 1989, p.42), and that young people should be in control of their own event.

The whole area of race provides a graphic example of the imperative of agreeing practice principles in advance of launching into intervention - the theme of this whole chapter. It is not good enough suddenly to recognise that the practice and organisational dilemmas of racist and sexist attitudes exist when these rise up in forms which can no longer be ignored. Workers in racially mixed or all white self-directed groups and projects need to think in advance, for example, about appropriate ways of challenging the racism of the white participants. Rhule (1988, p.44), offers an example of the role a consultant can play during the life of a group in helping workers to find appropiate times and methods of challenging racist remarks. This role can also be invaluable during the pre-planning stage, when the worker team needs to be reaching agreement that it will be its policy not to let comments go unchallenged and how to handle this in practice. For example, a commitment to confronting words must extend into actions and unspoken attitudes, and must never place the chief burden of doing all this on any black member(s) of the worker team. As Fine et al. (1985, p.57) state in this respect 'White people cannot leave the fight against racism to the racially oppressed. Racism is a white problem but it cannot be fought in isolated white movement' ... 'there must be autonomous black organisation but autonomy does not mean isolation'.

Accepting our own responsibility will push us as white workers into questioning our personal assumptions and stereotypes, and also needs to go further than this into addressing oppressive practice by those we work with, our white colleagues and management. Both organisations and individuals have to recognise and own the responsibility for positive action and change. Finally, workers need to look beyond the symptoms to tackling the causes of discrimination and oppression in wider society. Every organisation, worker team and group needs a statement embodying its commitment to anti-oppressive practice and this must, like all our underlying principles, be integral to our practice.

Gender
Most new entrants to the social work profession are able to offer a pretty fair analysis of gender oppression. Yet most practice remains sexist in its outcome. It still relies on armies of unpaid carers, still deals with women as mothers rather than as women - then blames them for their perceived inadequacies in the role, and still ignores the vast issues of domestic violence, of women's poverty, of the double oppression faced by black women, and so on. It is also sexist in its organisational structures and in their effects. Something is missing in most practice in the stage between analysis and action; the determination to challenge oppressive attitudes towards women which many practitioners profess as an ideal is failing to be carried through into practice.

Yet so much can be done from quite simple beginnings. First, groups of girls and of women need to be brought together to ask and answer the 'WHAT?', 'WHY?' and 'HOW?' questions (see Chapter Four) for themselves. In mixed groups, women talk less and typically look to the men's needs and to smoothing the way for them. In all female groups, their own interests can rise to the fore. A girls' group in a secondary school, just by watching videos together with skilled facilitation from a female worker, began to question the way women are seen in society, their own ambitions and their potential in life. A number of women, previously labelled as inadequate mothers, were brought together into a group and now run their own centre which offers a drop-in facility and all kinds of activities to numerous local women.

To take a more extended example, a social worker, working in conjunction with a voluntary sector youth work agency, became concerned about the isolation and lack of support for young women who had had babies while still at school. The young women were given the opportunity to discuss, in a group, issues which were important to them and to act on them if they wanted to. The topics they identified included housing, money, and their own futures. The discussion moved from each young woman's experiences to drawing out common problems and, from there, to the recognition of possible action they might take as a group. This included calling on a range of agencies, such as the housing, health and education authorities, to provide an effective response to their needs. They wanted the right to continue to receive schooling at the education department's special unit for pregnant school pupils after their babies were born, instead of having to choose between the embarrassment of returning to school or the possible disadvantages of leaving school early. They also felt it was unhelpful that those who returned to school had to do so full-time or not at all. The full school day could be problematic with a young baby and, of course, there was no creche provision there.

Although the workers, all women themselves, were experienced in girls' work, they encountered additional issues they had not anticipated because these particular group members all had very young children. Constant tiredness meant that the pace of the group and the length of concentration had to be adapted accordingly. The sheer motivation and organisation it took to get out of the house made attendance and continuity of membership problematic. The groupworkers questioned whether their own role should change to take account of the constant pressures on group members, either by taking more responsibility for group maintenance - such as remembering from week to week what topics the group had wanted to discuss - or for practical tasks such as (in the period before the group organised a creche for itself) feeding and changing the babies to free group members to concentrate on the work of the group.

In the same way that workers must challenge racism in their work, so it is important to ensure that sexism, both in workers and in service users, is recognised and tackled. A social action group, the Top End Youth Action Group (Social Action Training, 1989, pp.27-33) had submitted an Urban Aid application to run its own centre and was beginning to be taken more seriously in its local area. Alongside this, however, a problematic issue was bubbling in the group. The workers had been pointing out over a period of time that there were no girls in the group and that, if the group intended to represent the interests of all young people on the estate when the centre opened, then, on present showing, they would be no more than fifty per cent successful. On the surface, the members agreed, undertaking to talk to girls they knew and to put up posters seeking others to join the group. Their actions, however, were too little and too late to prevent the next development which was the sudden incursion into the middle of a group meeting of some girls and young women demanding to know why they were not represented on the Action Group. Whilst the workers were relieved to see them and warmly welcomed them in, the existing group members sat in sullen silence. They felt that 'their' territory was being invaded and did not intend to let it go without a fight. This marked the start of a protracted and bitter power struggle which ended with many of the young men withdrawing and the young women running the project.

During this period, the workers felt torn between Principle Two and Principle Five, that is, between their commitment to service users taking their own decisions and running their own group, on the one hand, and their determination to challenge sexism, on the other. Since both the existing, male, group members and the prospective, female, group members were service users, however, and since to side with the boys would have been to collude with oppression, the workers decided to support the girls' right to be heard and to join the group if they wanted to do so. In retrospect, they felt strongly that they should have challenged the issue of the absence of girls in the group far sooner, before the boys' position became entrenched.

A further example of tension between male and female group members, again where the workers backed the young women, comes from a group of Asian further education students who took up issues of institutional and personal racism with their College authorities. In this group, the female members said that the young men did not listen to them and insisted that sexism was as much a problem as racism. They took the initiative during one meeting to withdraw from the male members and the two workers (who were both Asian but both male), in order to discuss their needs on their own terms. They returned with a set of proposals which the group eventually accepted. Most important of these was the demand that, when the male student social worker left, the remaining male groupworker should be joined as co-worker by a female colleague from the Asian youth project which employed him. The workers were able to win agreement to this from the agency.

Class

In these days of emphasising racism and, to a lesser extent, sexism, class has become one of the most neglected issues in social work. Yet the majority of users of the social services continue to live in poverty (Becker and MacPherson, 1986). For practical purposes, class can seem an irrelevant category because welfare professionals do not set up groups specifically to work on class-based issues. Rather, many of the groups they work with consist of working class people, such as the housing estate-based groups mentioned elsewhere in this book and listed in the Appendix: the North Braunstone women's group (Donnelly, 1986), the Ainsley Teenage Action Group (for young people in trouble with the police), and the Rowland Dale Group for parents accused of abusing their children. Others, which cover a wider interest group, for example the Derbyshire Coalition of Disabled People find it crucial to include social class and material deprivation in their analysis of the issues confronting their members; even though this may lead to letters to their Newsletter Editor accusing the committee of being 'too political', and even though the membership includes people who are comfortably off, the group must tackle issues such as inadequate benefit levels for disabled people or miss a key factor which affects the life opportunities of many.

We do not count ourselves amongst those political activists who see social class as the single most important dividing factor, believing that it is only necessary for those who are oppressed on grounds of class to rise up for a new social order to be created. Rather, it seems clear that women, gay men and lesbians, black people, old and young people, and disabled people suffer oppression across class boundaries - though money can sometimes soften the blow - and will continue to do so unless all forms of oppression are acknowledged and tackled. By developing 'a theory of power rather than of the state', these and other forms of oppression can be revealed as significant factors (Rojek et al., 1988, p.99).

This does not, however, reduce class to just another category of oppression. To do so would leave the working class as a purely residual group - white, male and middle-aged. Rather, the dimensions must be seen to interlink in a much more complex way, each having the capacity to overarch several others at different times and in particular conditions, and needing to be confronted in a similarly interdependent way. For instance, if the particular point of struggle is in the work place over jobs then 'class action', in which power of labour confronts that of capital, rises to greatest significance (Fine et al., 1985, p.13). Alternatively, action may take place in the sphere of social provision, for instance over access to Rape Crisis Centres and Women's Aid Centres, as providing a means of protection in women's encounters with male violence, and a means of sustaining women's resistance against patriarchal oppression (Rowbotham et al., 1979). Failure to link the various dimensions, and simply to accept 'the idea of the trade union movement *as opposed* to the women's movement . . . *as opposed* to the anti-racism movement etc. . . . is to perpetuate the mythology and the strategy by which capitalism rules - that struggles are independent from each other and can be handled accordingly' (Fine et al., 1985, p.2).

It is on this basis that we have arrived at our value position and emergent understanding. Along with Webb (1985, p.94) we believe that there are points at which 'politico-ethical' purposes within the various dimensions coincide, and that the over-arching concepts and action themes of oppression and empowerment are just such a conjunction. Our concern in this book is to establish principles for practice and methods to implement these concepts, which are non-oppressive along all of these dimensions.

Age
In discussions of anti-oppressive working, it is relatively rare for age to receive more than lip-service.

> People are just beginning to have a glimpse of what oppression based on age involves. The fact is that our society is almost totally blind to the dignity and capacities of the very young and the very old. Children are like

women in being considered helpless, dependent, and cute
- creatures to be cherished and taken care of,

- or, we would add, abused within or beyond socially
constructed proprietorial 'rights' -

> but not full human beings to be deeply respected and trusted
> with significant power. . . . Older people are looked at as
> children - except that they often find themselves without
> anyone interested in cherishing or taking care of them.
> (Blood et al., 1983, p.7)

In the development of self-directed work, however,
considerations of age have always been at the forefront. As was
explained in Chapter One, it had important roots in social action
groups aimed at empowering young people, whose situation has
markedly worsened since then under the combined onslaughts of
government policies on benefits, housing, the poll tax, and so on.
It took place in the inner city, focusing on the interplay between
the material context of economic disadvantage and the social
context of young people's relative powerlessness in relationships
with adults (Ward, 1982a, p.6). Behaviour labelled as
'delinquency' was seen, not only as the result of repressive
attitudes towards young people expressed through heavy police
surveillance, but also as the response of working- class young
people to restricted social activities, owing to lack of money and
local facilities, as well as to their alienation from officially
sanctioned options. Social action practice concerns itself with all
these issues (Kearney and Keenan, 1988).

This involves accepting that: 'Conflicts with adults are . . . real
conflicts of interest and are not discounted as "acting out" '
(Ward, 1982a, p6). For many young people, their frustration
with the circumstances of their lives is equalled by their
alienation from, and lack of access to existing political and other
power structures (Kearney and Keenan, 1988, p.4). It is the
proper role of social action groupwork to support them in `tackling
all these facets of disempowerment'.

'Ageism' does not only affect young people. We consider that
oppressive attitudes based on chronology happen at both ends of
the age spectrum: elderly people, too, are commonly subjected to
stereotyping and oppressive views. Community action is by no
means unheard of among older citizens (Butcher et al., 1980,
pp.25-50; Phillipson, 1982, Chapter 8; Marshall, 1987), but we

have also come across some exciting examples of practice in mainstream welfare settings which rejects negative labels and, to varying degrees, moves towards empowering elderly service users.

Svedin and Gorosch-Tomlinson (1984) give an account of a luncheon club run by black elders. An encouraging beginning has also been made in a residential home where the officer-in-charge has actively rejected automatic assumptions about declining abilities and helped his staff team to work with residents' strengths. (See Mullender and Ward, 1985, for a more detailed account.) Although this has transformed the quality of care received by residents, it has not empowered them because they are by no means fully in control of what happens to them and cannot set their own goals for change. Also, although the officer-in-charge has arrived at clear views of his own about what was wrong, he has worked on a practice hunch in introducing change and has acted as an influential leader, rather than facilitator, within the home. Furthermore, residents themselves have not been encouraged to grow in awareness of the patronising and negative attitudes of others towards them by considering the way in which the dominant culture in British society treats its older members.

Other establishments have gone beyond this into full-blown self-advocacy with various kinds of residents' forums, and we have also come across an example of collective self-advocacy (Flower, 1983), based on the model of the National Association of Young People in Care, in which residents from all the elderly people's homes in one London borough had the chance to meet together and discuss their views on the quality of care they received. This was a most imaginative piece of work in that the special needs of this user group had to be considered in relation to concentration spans, hearing difficulties, and so forth. Where progressive senile decay makes self-representation problematic, self-advocacy can usefully be supplemented by citizen advocates who support individuals in expressing their concerns. Such a scheme has been developed in Warwickshire by Age Concern England (Greengross, 1988; Ellis, 1988) and parallels more widespread initiatives for people with learning difficulties and users of the mental health services (see below).

Disability

A similar range of critical work in empowerment, through

self-advocacy supported by citizen advocacy, has gone on in the field of disability.

Nottingham Patients Councils Support Group (NPCSG), for example, is an entirely user-run organisation which aims to establish collective forums (the patients councils) of service users to voice collective complaints and suggestions about hospital and day care services. Where these are not satisfactorily dealt with at ward or day centre level, and also where the future development of services is concerned, the group is instrumental in creating channels through which users can negotiate with management.

If we include under the heading of this section all conditions which are considered to be disabling, then a rich vein of groups can be listed here, including those concerned with physical disability (Derbyshire Coalition of Disabled People, 1986a and 1986b, and see Chapter Six), those for users and ex-users of the mental health services (Barker and Peck, 1987; Nottingham Patients Councils Support Group, 1989), and those for people with learning difficulties (Williams and Shoultz, 1982; *Enable* magazine). All are motivated by the same rejection of the view that people can be summed up by, or dismissed as a result of, some particular mental or bodily condition (Principle 1). They hold a view, instead, that it is social arrangements and attitudes which disable, through mechanisms such as segregation, isolation, and exclusion (Principle 3).

For some groups, the key challenge is to end the social marginalisation in special schools, hostels and day centres which, together with the constant impact of negative labelling, has told them that their views count for nothing. The office workers from *Enable* magazine, for example, who have all been labelled as having learning difficulties, jumped at the chance to be involved in a training day for social work students at the local University. The event was organised so that, rather than the visitors being set apart by making a 'presentation' about themselves and their work, the two groups met and worked together on an equal basis on the same activities. Every individual learned about everyone else present and their life experience, about their own collusion in perpetuating segregating myths and assumptions - based on their own fear of people different from themselves and counted as superior or inferior by the wider society - and about the nature of oppression: how and why it works, and how it can be tackled. In such ways, we can set in motion a process of reverse labelling for oppressed and segregated groups: the contribution of participants' positive qualities and achievements creates an upward spiral of positive recognition, self-belief and successful action, in place of the interplay of outside oppression, minimal expectations and low self-image which characterise the more usual, negative labelling process.

Other groups of people with learning difficulties have established user-led initiatives within the confines of specialist establishments and, through these, have still managed to create links with the 'non-disabled' world. The democratically elected student council at Avro Adult Training Centre, for example, persuaded the National Union of Students to allow and encourage those attending such centres to become NUS members (see Mullender and Ward, 1985, pp.166-167) - a similar reaching out by one group of learners to another as that of the *Enable* office workers.

Increasingly, the different user-led groups are breaking down the boundaries between physical and mental 'disabilities', not only because they have common experiences of labelling and inappropriate services, but because these boundaries exist in the categories of service offered and the budgets held by statutory authorities, and are not based on valid distinctions between individuals' own abilities or the services they personally may need. The Derbyshire Coalition, for example, has actively sought to make links with local groups of people with learning difficulties, and Nottingham Advocacy Group (for users and ex-users of the mental health services) has a person with learning difficulties on its Management Committee.

There is still further to go in seeing different forms of oppression as interlinked. It is not uncommon, when self-advocacy groups first start, for them to be more successful, initially, in empowering their white male members to speak out and to take on committee positions. Special efforts are often required to develop equal opportunities policies for these organisations, and to debate the issues, until white male participants recognise that the group is not speaking for its entire constituency until it gives an equal voice and equal representation to black people and women.

Sexual orientation
The gay and lesbian movement has given many, previously invisible people a voice, and mutually empowering attitudes and activities are at the heart of organisations of lesbians and of gay

men. So often, they have to provide these for themselves owing to the complete failure of the statutory agencies to do so:

> We are a youth group for teenagers who know they are homosexual or who think they are .... [T]he Youth Service. .. does not cater sufficiently for young gays. So, as there is a need for such a meeting place, we provide it for ourselves. (Annual report of a London-based youth group quoted in a *Youth in Society* publication, 1986, p.3)

Many local authorities' interpretation of section 28 of the Local Government Act, 1988, has ruled out answering the questions of young men and women who are confused about their sexuality, or meeting the needs of those of any age who are sure that their's does not conform to the heterosexual norm. Yet wishing the issue away colludes with homophobia and 'perpetuates the oppression, the prejudice and the discrimination' (*Youth in Society*, 1986, p.3).

Oppression of lesbians is additionally rooted in their visible rejection of dependency on men, the cornerstone of our patriarchal society. Nottingham Women's Centre has reserved one large, comfortable room solely for the use of lesbian groups. Heterosexual women may only go in at the invitation of lesbian users of the centre. The idea behind this is that, everywhere else they go, other than in the segregated, commercialised social and cultural outlets which profit by them, lesbians are made to answer for their sexuality and are prone to attack and ridicule. In this one place, they are guaranteed that, at any time, they can be themselves. It gives them a safe place from which to plan appropriate action for changing attitudes and service provision in the mainstream world beyond the women's centre.

As with the other forms of oppression, there is a need for growing awareness by such groups to be linked with a broader social analysis:

> Most large cities now have organised groups of young lesbians and young gay men ... Because of the position they have been placed in, they have had to think a great deal about themselves, about the meaning of sexuality, about the political systems that feed on prejudice and exclude minority groups, about traditional views of masculinity and femininity, about the ways in which young people are told what they can and cannot do by older and more powerful people. (Heaume, 1986, p.4)

In fact, as with every other form of oppression we have considered, the fight against homophobia must be shared - not just because it is the foundation of ugly forms of injustice (graphically illustrated, let us not forget, in the Nazi extermination of homosexual men and the characterisation of AIDS as the 'gay plague') but because, once again, the oppressions are closely interlinked: 'you don't have to be gay to support gay rights' (Kent-Baguley, 1986, p.9).

Conclusion

Through its explicit stating of essential principles, culminating in that of anti-oppressive working, the self-directed groupwork approach provides a common basis for practice and hence transcends the conventionally defined boundaries between disciplines such as social work, community work, youth work, teaching, adult education, community-based nursing, and others. Practitioners in any of these settings can work in an empowering way if they fashion their practice in ways which are congruent with an appropriate value-base, formulated within an understanding of wider political perspectives, and if they then translate its implications into their work. We have expressed our values as 'practice principles' which may be little more than a statement of intent. However, if that intent is given proper recognition as the core of practice, a clear statement of values can help transpose well intentioned, committed, but undisciplined work into a dynamic and refined approach which can, firstly, withstand evaluation and scrutiny and, secondly, sustain a clear commitment to social change objectives.

In the next chapter, we shall begin our detailed exploration of the difference these practice principles make to actual intervention.

Chapter Three

The Group Takes Off

In Chapter Two, we outlined the process of the workers preparing theselves for self-directed groupwork. In this chapter, the potential members come on the scene and we explore what happens when they come together with the workers to carry out the detailed planning for a group.

The key question throughout the next four chapters is: what difference do the values we outlined in Chapter Two make to practice? The answer, as far as this chapter is concerned, is that whereas, in most forms of traditional groupwork, the initial planning is done *on behalf of service users* , in self-directed action, the workers engage with users as partners to build a group, along open and user-led, rather than closed and worker-led, lines. This initiates an empowering style of work where users make key decisions such as whether to join the group, where and when to meet, and what arrangements will feel least oppressive. A new style of '*open planning*', as we have called it (Mullender and Ward, 1989), has to be developed in order for user-led action to ensue.

Making Planning *Em*-powering: A Detailed Examination of Stage 'B' of the Self-Directed Model

We have worked with many practitioners now, in different countries, on unlearning and rethinking their ideas on planning. We use exercises which can also be used by worker teams with their consultants to thrash out their values prior to starting work in order to ensure that they have a clear agreement about the model of planning they will adopt and about its compatibility with the self-directed approach. The technique we use is to invite workers to adopt a completely polarised approach: to think about the extremes on a continuum of open and of closed - or, we might say, of empowering and of disempowering - planning.

They are firstly invited to consider how many of the items on conventional planning lists could, in fact, be postponed until service users can be involved. In other words, what is the bottom-line in advance planning? Of course the worker or worker team has to decide on an interest in groupwork and carry out their own pre-planning as mentioned in the last chapter. Other than this, the only work which absolutely needs to be done in advance of convening service users is to discuss with potentially interested parties:

1. whether there is sufficient reason to call a meeting and what a possible group might do (potential **goals**),
2. who is interested enough to attend once and give the group a try (potential **membership**),
3. a place for a first meeting (**venue**),
4. a time for a first meeting (issues of **timing**).

Thought also needs to be given to how to let people know about the first meeting, and how to handle that first occasion when people need to be put at their ease, for example with refreshments, but will want to leave feeling a sense of purpose and the viability of change (Burghardt, 1982, p.59). Arrangements for any further meetings (such as venue, timing and activities) need not be fixed in advance by the workers; it is more empowering if they are jointly discussed and agreed by workers and participants when the group first comes together.

Even the decisions listed above are best made through a process of prior discussion with the individuals who might wish to attend. Thus, the idea for the group should have arisen from contact with service users. There needs to be a shared feeling that something needs changing, held by a core of people who are willing to attend a first meeting. This view can then be floated with others to see if they agree, and whether they are prepared to come along and add their strengths to the combined effort for change. General views can also be sought on a good time and place to hold the meeting, how best to publicise it - who needs to be told and where are people likely to see posters? - and other details about the arrangements, such as whether a creche will be needed. This can be helpful in checking out that people will not be kept away at this early stage by not having heard about the meeting, by domestic commitments, by feeling uncomfortable or out-of-place in the suggested venue (it should be 'a safe place with good vibrations' as one workshop member put it), or by not being able to manage the proposed time.

As well as giving their own explanations of why the meeting has been called, the workers may well be able to involve service users in addressing the meeting to outline what concerns they have and why they decided to attend. Members of existing groups with similar concerns and successes already under their belt can also be effective speakers. The Nottingham Who Cares Group had a speaker from the National Association of Young People in Care at its inaugural meeting who outlined the tremendous strides that organisation had made. The only draw-back was that his involvement in NAYPIC had made him such a poised and self- confident seventeen year-old, that those attending the meeting found him hard to identify with; they thought he was a social worker! At a first meeting, members will begin to decide whether they accept the workers as facilitators and themselves as capable of self-direction, whilst workers encourage and support members' early testing of their own and workers' attitudes and early initiatives in articulating their views and feelings.

Next, in the workshops we run, we encourage the professionals present to consider first how one could set up a group in the most *dis*-empowering way imaginable. Once the small groups' 'disempowering' lists are assembled and written up, from ceiling to floor down the left-hand side of a roll of newsprint paper, we ask them to work back down the list and work out what the opposite of each item would be - i.e. how they could initiate a group or project in the most *em*-powering way possible.

Naturally, the lists which have resulted from these fairly light-hearted workshop sessions are exaggerated - caricatures, even - and it is not our intention to suggest that anyone would deliberately set out to work in an overtly disempowering way. To their surprise, however, the workshop participants conclude that there is more than a grain of resemblance between the left-hand, 'disempowering' list they have drawn up and their own practice. They find it liberating to consider afresh just how much of traditional, worker-led planning (see, for example, Douglas, 1976, pp.41-42) can be replaced by shared deliberations with intending members about the style and shape they would like their new group to take.

What follows is a compilation of some of the workshop responses on empowering and disempowering planning and an exploration in greater depth of the ideas on what can make planning empowering (the right-hand column in each case). We shall look in greater detail at the effect of keeping the process as open, uncommitted and participative as possible, rather than pre-ordained and heavily worker-led.

Reason to Hold a Group - Potential Goals

Disempowering Approach	Empowering Approach
The boss thinks it's a good idea	Workers acknowledge and contract to work with a pre-existing group on members' own issues
or	**or**
I think it's a good idea/worker's pet project	alternatively, idea arises from one or more potential members and is checked out by the workers with others who might like to join
Student on placement is required to run a group as determined by the agency	Student holds to own value position and follows one of the above routes into groupwork
Goals pre-set by workers/imposed on group	Goals set by group

Discussion

PRE-EXISTING GROUPS

Not a little self-directed action takes place in 'natural' groups, that is in groups which are not brought together by professionals. Practitioners all too often have a tendency to ride roughshod over such groups - even to fail to recognise that they exist - because they do not fit into the neat categories of case allocation and planning which are employed in the average statutory agency.

An example of where this 'top-down' tendency was avoided was in relation to the Ainsley Teenage Action Group. Here, a probation officer who received a number of individual referrals to prepare court reports on young people accused of offences which had all been committed on a particular council estate, recognised that these young people already constituted a natural friendship group which could be a source of mutual support and strength. He determined to work with the group of young people as a group instead of splitting them up and seeing them individually.

IDEA ARISING FROM MEMBERS

Even where a group does not already exist, the idea may arise in the normal course of discussion with service users or local people in a neighbourhood. Perhaps a problem appears to be particularly widespread in one district or a significant number of people have all mentioned the same area of worry or discontent. The worker's attention is drawn to the issue and he or she raises it with other local people, seen during the normal course of professional practice in that locality. Gradually a picture emerges of an issue which is causing undue concern and which sufficient people feel motivated to tackle to make it worthwhile to call a preliminary meeting. Potential members of a group, or activists in a campaign, put out feelers to others to gauge the strength of feeling and level of interest in doing something about it. The worker's task is to facilitate and participate in this process; to ease and assist communication, perhaps to help in suggesting or providing a meeting-place, and so on. It is not to determine the focus of intervention in the role of expert on other people's problems.

STUDENT INVOLVEMENT IN GROUPWORK

It is not uncommon for students to want to, or to be required to 'get some groupwork experience'. Our expectation of students would be akin to our expectation of any other practitioners: that they should develop a clear value-base before launching into practice and that their work should flow from this.

GOAL-SETTING BY THE GROUP

Leaving aside the question of the need to set goals - which we would suggest holds true for any model of groupwork - the issue of who sets the goals for the group forms one facet of Principle 2 in the value-base set out in Chapter Two: that people must have control over their own agenda of action. It also brings us to the heart of open planning. Goals constitute the crucial area of deliberation which must be undertaken by the participants themselves, with the facilitation of the workers, as opposed to being pre-determined by the professionals and imposed on the service users. Most social workers are accustomed to deciding the goals for a group in advance. Teachers and health professionals would also typically work in this way, whereas community workers might vary between more and less directive styles of working. Where practitioners are so used to setting goals, they come to see this as inevitable and as necessary for the functioning of the group - otherwise why would anyone want to attend?

In fact, the experience of self-directed workers has been that a shared area of oppression or of concern, and the wish to discuss it and see if any action is possible, are enough to bring potential members together. The workers obviously have an overarching purpose in involving themselves in assisting this to happen, but this is the general one of empowering people to seek their own solutions to wider social problems. For workers to go beyond this into dictating detailed goals to the group would take away the ownership of the group and its efforts from group members. Only the members have had the life experiences which legitimate their establishment of aims and priorities within the group. The workers' role is to facilitate them in this.

Not only must the latter formulate their own goals, but the workers must actively accept these goals as their own and not merely appear to do so while in fact clinging to hidden agendas. Goals can take a good few meetings to emerge and hence take us beyond the proper content of this chapter, which concerns itself with planning for the work. There will, of course, be a process of discussion and negotiation within the group, once it is launched, in which the workers can participate to facilitate the process but not to guide the outcome.

Membership

Disempowering	Empowering
Membership is restricted by referral and selection	Group is widely advertised and invitations are also dispersed by word of mouth; there is no selection stage
Members are deterred from joining because race and gender issues are ignored	Potential black and/or women members are given clear 'signals' that their experience in the group will not be racist or sexist
Numbers are limited by selection process	Numbers fluctuate, with no minimum or maximum group size, owing to:
Closed membership imposed by the worker	Open-ended membership. Participants can join or leave at any time
Compulsory membership	Voluntary membership

Discussion

Non-selected membership with wide publicity

Open planning does not involve setting criteria for membership or taking referrals. Potential members are simply invited along on the basis of a shared problem, or they see the group or project advertised, or someone tells them about it and they decide to go along and give it a try. There may be a two-stage process involved, in that a worker may spread the idea of a potential group partly to see if there is likely to be any take-up for it. In responding positively, potential participants are indicating both their own interest and the viability and validity of the project itself. In this way, a new idea may be 'seeded' to see if it takes root.

Although members may have heard about the group initially through their social workers or health visitors, or through any other professionals who have a significant involvement in their lives, they cannot be 'referred' as such - the group is merely suggested to them for their own consideration as a potentially useful or interesting idea. Whilst it is not associated with any process of selection, many self-directed groupworkers do, nevertheless, meet potential members individually before the group starts. What workers will be exploring is that this will be *their* group or project in which they will meet others - or be with others they already know - who are facing similar problems to their own, and that the workers will only be there to help them discuss what form the problems take, which of them are experienced as the most severe, why these problems exist and how, as a group, they might choose to tackle them.

ATTRACTING BLACK AND WOMEN MEMBERS

Open membership is not really 'open' if whole categories of people stay away. In order to attract black members to a mixed group, for instance (where this is appropriate), not only will the workers need to think about the overall racial balance and avoid a tokenistic black presence in ones or twos; they will also need to make it publically clear that they have thought about and acted on issues of racism. As Thomas (1986, p.143) puts it, they must 'signal that they offer a different experience'. Muston and Weinstein (1988, pp.35-36) offer pointers to workers in mixed race groups on how to offer an appropriate group experience to black participants. These include the issues of composition of and external support to the worker team, group content, early acknowledgement in the group of the racial mix and the possibility of racism, challenging denial by the white members, working with distrust and negative feelings, and not using black members as cultural experts. Unless these intentions are flagged in advance, potential black members are justified in expecting the usual, structurally and individually racist response from a predominantly white agency and may well see no point in subjecting themselves to attending. (See also Davis, 1984.)

Other potential black members of mixed or same-race groups, who are simply never reached by the prevailing 'colour-blind' services, will remain untouched by any new initiative unless the changes include more appropriate methods of outreach and publicity. These may include the use of locally-spoken languages, the ethnic press, and a completely different set of networks from those habitually used. Black members will often be far readier to join an all-black group, in which they know they will find a black perspective, than any other. Muston and Weinstein (1988, p.33, drawing on Eytle, 1985) give an example of a black student who established a black pensioners' group. Her agency had tried to tell her that there were few black pensioners on the estate, that black elders would not need a group, and that there was no need for a specifically black group. In fact, she contacted a local doctor who immediately identified fifteen people who could potentially benefit greatly from a group but who, since they were, in the main, not using existing, white services were 'officially invisible' (op. cit.).

Potential women members, likewise, may well have had bad experiences of agencies who blame them for failing to maintain officially sanctioned standards as mothers or exploit them as unpaid carers. They may require proof that their experiences will be listened to and understood before they trust the group to meet their needs. The latter will always be far easier in an all-female environment. Moyer and Tuttle's interesting paper (1983) on 'Overcoming Masculine Oppression in Mixed Groups', however, offers check-lists on 'Common Pitfalls' and on 'Becoming Responsible' which could be of great help both in challenging male group members not to silence women and to workers of both sexes in mixed groups not to let this happen. (See also Martin and Shanahan, 1983, and other papers in Garvin and Reed, 1983.)

The best form of proof that any group intends to provide an appropriate service to women is practical provision: of creche facilities or dependency expenses, for example. The language that is used to describe the group in prior publicity - as a mothers' group or a women's group? - will also be important. In addition, all the other aspects of planning come together to constitute an 'appropriate' service for women. The fact that members set their own goals on their own terms - campaigning for a day nursery, not 'working with inadequate mothers to raise standards of child care' - and that women are not belittled or over-ridden by workers concerned with different agendas, are signposts women know how to read.

FLUCTUATING GROUP SIZE

It is obviously not empowering to deny someone access to a group or project which is relevant to their life experience and which they are interested in joining. Yet, since encouraging their attendance means leaving membership unselected and open, the workers will later be faced with complete uncertainty about attendance at any particular meeting. The number of participants will inevitably fluctuate over time and there may be stages when it is very large. This can lead practitioners, particularly social workers, into unfamiliar territory; their previous practice, like the literature on groupwork, is likely to have been based around the narrow band of group membership ranging from three, or ideally from six, to twelve members (Brown et al., 1982, p.589). Youth workers, community workers, and most people who operate in residential and educational settings will be used to dealing with larger numbers but not necessarily to involving them all in a process of change.

Social workers, particularly, may feel tempted to edge the group towards a size which feels safer and more familiar, or to work with subgroups of the whole in the belief that this is the only workable option: 'The tendency to sub-grouping can be used constructively by sub-dividing the group for various tasks and activities' (Brown, 1986, p.41). Stock Whitaker (1975, p.434) similarly advises that: 'A group of 12 or 15 or more is too large for many purposes . . . groups of this size almost always devolve into a small core of active participants and a fringe of onlookers' - although she does go on to add that large groups may be desirable in certain residential or hospital ward settings, simply so that everyone can be included. Preston-Shoot (1987, p.32) considers that members themselves may also find size problematic, fearing that, in big groups, both intimacy and freedom of expression will be threatened and tasks less efficiently carried out, though there will be more experience and creative energy available. The latter point reflects Brown's concession to the positives of higher numbers (1986, p.40): 'For problem-solving, activity and "open" groups, larger groups provide more resources and can work well'.

In self-directed contexts, since no upper limit is set on attendance, it is not uncommon to find numbers in excess of twenty, and forty is not unheard of. An Asian students' group at a further education college and the Nottingham 'Who Cares' Group for young people in care certainly both exceeded twenty members at times and both benefited from their wealth of ideas and talents. The workers with these groups had to find the skills from somewhere to involve everyone in discussion and planning, without resorting to formal committee structures that would have been quite inappropriate. There was little assistance to be derived from the existing literature. With the exception of Kreeger (1973), the theoretical literature on groups of this dimension tends to be out of harmony with the self-directed orientation towards social action. (See, for example, Jones, 1953, and Bozarth, 1981.)

We would add that there are particular techniques which can draw well attended groups into discussions which deliberately and safely involve everyone - thus allowing the group to benefit from the larger numbers present - which do not pander to the loudest voices but allow for differing views to be heard, and which result in the group's work being efficiently carried out. They include exercises designed to raise a wide range of issues, such as brainstorming, others aimed at sifting and prioritising the resulting ideas and setting tasks arising from them, and games designed to help the group look at its own process. (Examples of all these may be found in the following chapters.)

At other times in self-directed contexts, when only a few members are present, it is important not to retreat into feeling that they represent a more 'authentic' small group and to treat them as if they *were* the whole group by letting them take fresh decisions in contravention of all the work done thus far. One way of holding on to what the large group has set as its priorities is to display its work to date at every meeting, and to keep that in the forefront as representing the direction in which the group is aiming to move. The contribution and views of all are thus acknowledged and built on.

Self-directed groups may go through periods of feeling that numbers have shrunk too far and decide to publicise the group to attract more members. This may be done through word of mouth when, for example in young people's groups, members will bring their friends along to the next meeting. Alternatively, a group may consider putting posters up in its usual meeting place, or may even advertise in the press, as the Rowland Dale Group for parents accused of abusing their children considered doing when it needed more members to help it run independently of worker support.

Open Membership

It is appropriate that members should opt in and out of self-directed groups as they feel able to make the commitment of their time or when they experience the issues at stake as touching on their own current concerns. This can be very positive for the group since success is closely tied to motivation. Someone whose attention is preoccupied with debts or domestic problems, or who has simply moved on to other things, will not feel inclined to stay and give their best to the group, whereas others with a key contribution to make may respond to renewed publicity or be encouraged to join by remaining members.

Although Galinsky and Schopler (1985) have shown that, in practice, open groups are not uncommon, the majority of mainstream theorists on groupwork appear biased in favour of closed groups: 'A closed group does seem to promote cohesion and trust and may provide security for members who initially are apprehensive or lacking in confidence' (Preston-Shoot, 1987, p. 31).

Michael Henry (1988, pp.216-217), on the other hand, sees potential benefits for participants in open membership. Though these are all expressed in therapeutic terms, some can be applied to a self-directed model, notably his notion of members seeing that change is possible in the example of others who are at more advanced stages of personal development - new members of our groups see change as possible because of what the *group* has achieved. Henry (ibid., pp.218-219) also mentions sources (Hill and Gruner, 1973; Bailis et al., 1978; Sue Henry, 1981) which show that groups do not become stuck because of the constant arrivals, but pass progress on from generation to generation. They retain a central 'essence' of goals, norms and shared history. In addition, a core of the membership itself often remains involved over a long period. All these features are true of self-directed groups and will be explored elsewhere in this book. If it is clearly built in from the beginning, we would maintain that a turnover of membership can be well handled - by ensuring full discussion of the changes in the group, and sharing responsibility between workers and members for handling the welcoming and leaving process. As regards the advent of new members, most open groups take this in their stride and welcome the potentially valuable contribution that new members may make to their collective efforts. An appropriate way of involving them can be through making a clear presentation of group goals and work achieved to date - with the proviso that they can certainly have a role in further shaping these.

An area of difficulty can arise when the group has become rather 'cliquey' after a period when membership has remained unchanged. On the whole, though, members know why they themselves chose to join and why they have found the group useful, so discussion will usually reawake the conviction that others facing similar difficulties should also have that option. In an open-ended model, departures will not be unexpected and the workers can enable full discussion of the feelings they evoke. If members have become important to one another, they can continue to meet outside the group. Only if anyone opts out of the group with bad feeling is the group likely to need to discuss their departure at length. Since we believe that members should not just 'disappear' under these circumstances, and since their going can sometimes be a clear indication of barely submerged rumblings amongst members, here again, workers should facilitate full discussion of what has happened.

VOLUNTARY MEMBERSHIP

No doubt members of groups which they have been obliged to attend can, on occasions, find the experience empowering once they have made their own decision to opt into what the group is doing. The fact of compulsion itself, however, is normally profoundly disempowering and, as a worker wishing to practise empowerment, one would seriously want to question the reason for it before giving oneself such an initial stumbling-block. We do not consider it to be viable for members to feel that the group and its goals belong to them if they have been required to attend.

Self-directed practice *has* been shown to be workable alongside statutory involvement, however. Membership of a self-directed group is not precluded for those on court orders, or those subject to statutory monitoring or investigation, provided that there is no actual or implied requirement that they will join the group. This is of crucial importance in self-directed groupwork since the right to decide whether or not to participate is an essential feature of Principle 2 of the value-base underlying the approach (cf Chapter Two).

So how can statutory controls and voluntary membership be reconciled? A helpful consideration here is the differentiation made by Bottoms and McWilliams (1979, p.177) between constraint and coercion. Coercion, they argue, is unacceptable, whereas constraints exist in all situations in which people interact. They merely provide a framework within which real choice remains possible. This notion of choice can be further developed by considering the idea of contracts (Mullender, 1979). 'Even where statute limits users' rights, and the freedom of social workers, contracts will identify the extent of their freedom and power' (Preston-Shoot, 1989, p.43) and, applying this to groupwork, 'These approaches enable members to participate actively in devising and running the group, and to make an informed choice about membership' (ibid., p.44).

A primary contract, the order, provides a framework such as the requirement in a probation or supervision order to report regularly (Bryant et al., 1978). Beyond this framework, the person who is subject to the order remains free to choose whether to enter into one or more secondary contracts, which may include receiving individual help through casework or joining a group. In the Ainsley Teenage Action Group, for example, the probation officer who set up the group gave members the option of fulfilling the reporting requirement of their orders by attending the group. He made it clear that, should they withdraw from the group, their primary contract - the statutory order - would not be broken, provided that they worked out an alternative arrangement for contact. Since subsequent withdrawal from a secondary contract would not prejudice the conditions of the court order (which remains in force), the existence of the order itself does not prevent potential group members from exercising a real choice.

Venue and Access

Disempowering	Empowering
Stairs only access/ Communication obstacles	Lift access/accessible toilets/etc. Induction loops/braille facilities/ BSL interpreters.
No creche	Creche
Office of statutory agency Hard to get to/hard to find	On group's own territory **or** in appropriate setting on neutral ground in members' own community
Members are transported by workers in agency vehicles	Members make their own way

Discussion
ACCESS

There is nothing more profoundly disempowering than arriving at the foot of a flight of stairs which you are unable to climb. Nor, in this day and age, is it any longer acceptable to telephone a venue and ask if is accessible for disabled people and to receive a reply in the affirmative, only to arrive and discover that they meant someone would be available to carry you in - as happened to a friend recently at a *social work* conference! Surely we should know better by now?

As that example shows, the attempt by able-bodied people to anticipate disabled people's needs can be very misleading and only a true process of consultation with disabled people themselves is genuinely reliable and empowering. It is so easy to be caught out. The main doorway may look wide enough, but there may not be a toilet which is actually accessible in a wheelchair. It is not only those who try to attend the group or take part in the project or conference who are liable to be disempowered. Even more serious, perhaps, is the issue of those who never even try to attend because they assume their needs will not be met. It is one thing to seek a British sign-language interpreter or a braille machine after the lack of suitable communication techniques has become glaringly obvious. It is quite another to take appropriate advice beforehand and advertise the group as welcoming people with communication disabilities. As with gender and race issues (see above), it is necessary to announce publically that this group is different from all the tired old disempowering practice.

CRECHES: THE RECOGNITION OF DOMESTIC RESPONSIBILITIES

In just the same way, people with child care responsibilities may automatically rule themselves out of meetings if no provision is made to meet their needs , for example by offering a creche. If their presence is excluded by practical obstacles they may assume from this that they themselves are not wanted or are considered to have nothing to offer: 'Oh, I'm just a housewife!'. As with disabled people, the only truly empowering course is to consult potential users themselves as to their actual needs, A particular child may not be able to adjust to the strange adults or children in a creche, but an offer to pay for child care arrangements which the mother herself makes may solve the problem of how to attend the group.

There are two glaring omissions in the preceding sentence. One is fathers, and the other the carers of other dependent relatives besides young children. Only carers' groups typically think about the latter point. Whereas everyone would be familiar with the idea, if not with the practicalities of straightforward creche provision, most workers would not know what services are available or required by other groups such as sufferers from senile dementia or children with learning difficulties. Such is the neglect, that the self-directed group is likely to have to take up the campaign of fighting to get appropriate respite services provided, as opposed to simply finding out what exists and putting potential members in touch.

ON GROUP'S OWN TERRITORY . . .

In that open planning means involving members in deciding what they want their group to be like, this can also be extended to choosing the most appropriate location for group meetings. They may, in fact, be indicating this through the places where they tend to congregate naturally, such as the members of a group of Asian students from a further education college who spent a lot of time in the library because their parents approved of it but they could still see their friends there. It can be patronising to assume without asking, however, that they are where they ideally want to be, as opposed to where they feel forced to be through lack of any alternative.

With young people, for example, the most natural setting in which to find them initially could be a street corner or a public open space of some kind and work with them may have to be started there if it is to start at all. We often give the example of a detached youth worker who was very skilled in self-directed groupwork techniques doing precisely this when he came across a natural group of young people 'hanging around' on a housing estate. Wanting to encourage them to voice their own experiences of living on the estate, he proceeded to pull a piece of chalk out of his jacket pocket and to hold a 'brainstorming' session with them there and then, by writing on the paving stones. This led to the group negotiating for somewhere to meet. They had previously felt alienated from all the obvious adult-run and adult-sanctioned alternatives, such as the local youth club, but it became a matter of considerable pride to book a room entirely for their own use in a community centre or, as the Asian students did, in their own college or school.

Existing locations of pre-existing groups may also be used in residential, day care and ward settings. The use of self-directed groupwork in penal settings (Badham, 1989) should remind us, however, that a group's everyday setting is not necessarily one in which it feels perfectly at ease. One way round this is to 'customise' the surroundings and make them feel more like the group's own territory. This can either be done just for group meetings if the prevailing climate is an unchangeably hostile or authoritarian one - by putting up the group's flip charts, for example, and re-arranging the furniture - or it may be a permanent adaptation, such as pressing for members to be allowed to choose the decor in a day centre.

.. OR ON NEUTRAL TERRITORY IN MEMBERS' OWN COMMUNITY

Where individual members are being brought together for the express purpose of starting a self-directed group and there is, therefore, a completely open choice of venue, the initial one or two meetings should normally be held on 'neutral' territory such as a community centre, away from the professionals' normal workplaces, and the preferred location of future meetings discussed with those members who come along at this initial stage. The setting must be appropriate for the type of group and they have to feel happy in it: a large, bare room may look uninviting to middle-class professionals but may feel ideal to a group of boisterous young people who do not want to be accused of damaging anything. Once again, we are emphasising that no aspect of planning should unnecessarily be taken out of group members' hands.

TRANSPORT

It is not normally appropriate for workers to provide transport to a self-directed group because it influences people to attend when they may not want to make the commitment or may have other priorities. It is questionable as to how far attendance remains truly voluntary when transport arrives without fail every week; it is easier to attend by default than to send the driver away. There would have to be some special reason to provide it, for example if members are disabled and require help. Even then, they may well be able to find their own community transport and book a seat on it only when they choose to. The issue of stigmatising labels on 'official' vehicles is an international one. State wards (young people in care) in New Zealand won their battle to have the words emblazoned down the side of Department of Social Welfare cars removed. They were replaced with small windscreen stickers for insurance and identification purposes only.

Timing, frequency and overall number of meetings

Disempowering	Empowering
All fixed by worker/inconvenient	All decided by agreement/ mutually convenient

Discussion

TIMING OF MEETINGS - WHO DECIDES AND FOR WHOSE BENEFIT?

Similar principles relate to the timing of meetings as to every other issue over which workers have traditionally taken charge but in relation to which the self-directed approach advocates member involvement. Brown (1986, p.41) rightly regards discussing meeting times with members as desirable within many approaches to groupwork; we would not claim this as specific to our work. It is of particular importance there, however, because it relates to Principle 2: members choosing the kind of intervention they find acceptable and being in control of it.

FREQUENCY OF MEETINGS

Once again, the frequency of meetings constitutes a feature which is not fixed in advance in self-directed groupwork. There is a tendency, in adult-led long-term groups, to assume that meetings will take place once a month, whilst short-term groups may well meet weekly. In self-directed groups there is a far greater element of the members determining what feels right for them and what will best enable them to meet the group goals they have set.

Again, to take the Nottingham 'Who Cares' group as an example, the groupworkers - who were new to the self-directed approach - had made the assumption in advance, following the model of most adult meetings, that the group would meet monthly. After the group had actually started, the members - all teenagers in foster care and residential care - stated that they would prefer to meet weekly. It seems likely that they were more accustomed to weekly groups, on the model of Scouts or Guides for example. They also found it easier and more realistic to plan their lives a week rather than a month ahead. The reasons for this included the routines established within the children's homes where most of them lived, their schools' weekly schedules of homework and of out-of-school commitments such as team sports, their own sense of time which revolved around a somewhat shorter timescale than that of adults, and their vague awareness that control over their use of time, and even over where they might be a few months hence, was not in their own hands - which made it important to achieve as much as possible as quickly as possible. The lack of fit between the group leaders' expectations of monthly meetings and the members' wish for weekly meetings led to a compromise that the group would meet fortnightly. This suited no-one particularly well, did not harmonise with anyone's other commitments so that it became difficult to remember the meeting dates, and caused problems in fitting meetings around holidays and half-terms.

Open-Ended Length of Group

Just as the number attending a self-directed group is not fixed in advance, so the workers need to learn not to pre-set the duration of time during which the group will meet. It is not easy to move away from the kind of 'gut level' feeling in many professional settings which has come to associate small groups with a typically time-limited duration of six to twelve meetings (Brown et al., 1982, p.591). More practice is undertaken in groups of open-ended length than is commonly recognised, usually associated with open membership (Henry, 1988).

Often, however, time-spans are calculated according to the length of commitment workers feel they can make, rather than the exigencies of the group itself. This is compounded by the unfortunate tendency to regard any form of 'self-help' activity as able to become member-led after a very short period of time (Wilson, 1987) so that, again, the pressure is towards workers' own involvement in the group lasting perhaps only a matter of weeks. In self-directed groupwork, group members themselves decide for how long they find the group to be serving a useful purpose, which frequently extends over a period of years until long-term goals for external change are achieved.

Groupworkers may hand the responsibility for facilitating the group in its work over to colleagues after a time (subject to the group's agreement), or eventually over to members themselves, but workers should not expect to be associated with the group for less than a good few months - and years would be better. Such a long-term commitment makes a team of at least three workers especially desirable, so that sickness and leave can be covered. These workers need not all be from the same agency - for example, the facilitators with the Rowland Dale Group were a social worker and a health visitor.

The Three 'R's: Rules, Recording and Worker Roles

Once a group has come together, as well as the group members deciding for themselves whether they want to attend, making the planning decisions such as where and when to meet in future, and taking responsibility, as a group, for setting the group's goals, there are a number of other matters to be decided. Once again, they need to reflect maximum involvement of, and control by, group members.

Self-directed groupwork is grounded in the notion of a working agreement (Brown, 1986, pp.44-46) between workers and members. In the earliest stages of a group's life, this agreement will focus on the facilitative rather than leadership nature of the workers' roles. The expectations of members on first joining the group will need to be explored and clarified, as would be the case with any method. It will need to be clear from the start that they will not be telling members what to do but will be handing the responsibility for decisions to them. In addition, the working agreement needs to cover any rules for the conduct of the group, including those relating to confidentiality; who 'owns' and records information about the group and its achievements; and the roles which groupworkers play in relation to those group members who are receiving individual help alongside group membership (including any with a statutory component). These latter points can be summed up under the three 'R's of Rules, Recording, and Roles of workers who are involved both in individual and in group work.

Rules

Whereas, in conventional groupwork, it may be appropriate to have rules imposed by workers, rules and norms for the conduct of self-directed groups are collectively determined and recognised by the members, in ways which the group itself decides, such as a majority vote or reaching a consensus view. Typical early examples of decisions which the whole group can be encouraged to take together, and which can involve important lessons for members in working co-operatively, include choosing a name for the group - which also asserts the members' 'ownership' of the group. Many groups quickly decide on a rule that chairing will be exercised in a non-hierarchical style and that it will rotate around the group. This gives everyone a chance to learn the skills involved and prevents control being vested too strongly with any one individual (Freeman, 1970). Groups need to establish their own statement to cover anti-oppressive aims in their working principles, since they will not automatically regard themselves as covered by those the worker team has agreed on in its pre-planning phase. Issues concerning group decisions about who may join or who is asked to leave have already been touched on in earlier sections under membership. Decisions about control over the budget and spending decisions also need to be taken by the group as a whole. Young people's groups may encounter particular issues here, in not being trusted with public money by funders (Harrison, 1982, p.24) or not being allowed to hold an account in their own name with signatories aged under 18. Adult-run organisations, such as banks, may find the principles on which the group operates hard to understand and may look to the workers to exercise adult control.

Groups need to establish ways whereby everyone's contribution is valued and everyone has an equal right to participate fully in the meetings. Some participants will have strengths in carrying out tasks and others in studying and reflecting on group process. Status should not reside in how loudly people can shout. In the Nottingham 'Who Cares' Group, for example, after one or two rather boisterous and noisy meetings the young people themselves decided on the rule that only one person should speak at once and that the others should listen. It would, of course, have been perfectly possible for the workers to predict that such a rule would be needed and to have delivered it to members as an expectation at the first meeting. This, however, would have established a 'them and us' feeling between workers and members and would have placed the former firmly in a leadership role. When the groupworkers had later gone on to say to members 'This is your group and it is up to you to decide how you want to use it and what you want to achieve', the members would have had no reason to believe that this was actually how the workers intended to operate.

The same 'Who Cares' group also had to tackle the issue of confidentiality between the group and the outside world. The residential staff who were caring for most of the young people felt somewhat threatened by the existence of the group and would sometimes 'pump' them for information as to what went on there. The group considered this situation and reached the opinion that they had a right to discuss matters which concerned them in privacy but that, at the same time, there was no point in fostering suspicion of the group's activities unnecessarily. As a result, the members decided that they needed a rule that the content of group sessions was confidential. Such freedom was absolutely essential if they were to have the necessary space to share their adverse experiences of the care system and to reach decisions on how to tackle these. The groupworkers regarded themselves as bound by exactly the same expectations. So as not to feel that they were being disloyal to individual social workers or carers, however, they further decided to hold occasional 'open evenings' for their field and residential social workers at which the group's progress and plans could be reported on. In this way, the whole group would have a chance to plan what would be shared and how, and, at the same time, support could be enlisted for the group's continued existence from a group of significant adults.

A different aspect of confidentiality, that between workers and members, was faced by the Ainsley Teenage Action Group (a fuller account of whose work appears in Chapter Five). The worker team with this group was meeting regularly with a consultant to help them keep in view their overall philosophy of empowerment of the young people in the group, and to develop the kinds of skills and techniques which would make this a reality. When the existence of these consultancy sessions first came up in conversation between the workers and the young people, the latter were angry that there were discussions going on about *their* group from which they felt excluded, in just the same way as the residential workers had felt shut out from the 'Who Cares' group. In this case, however, the fact that it was the members of the group themselves who were experiencing this feeling of exclusion raised a very real dilemma for the worker team. Workers and members together discussed the situation, with the groupworkers strongly holding the opinion that they had a right to their own professional development and, indeed, that they could not offer an adequate service to the group without it. On the other hand, they did not want to create any 'no go' areas in their work, nor to leave the members feeling that they were being talked about behind their backs. The group decided that the workers did have a right to, and a need for, time and space for their own reflection but that this should not be kept confidential from group members. It was also agreed that any members who wished to do so would be free to attend the consultancy sessions, that the focus of these should remain on the performance of the workers, and that they would not develop into mini-group sessions outside of the meetings proper. In addition, the records of the consultancy sessions would be open to the group members to read. Members increasingly became able to offer their own feedback to workers in these sessions and elsewhere, as is normal in the evaluation of self-directed groups (see Chapter Six).

Whatever rules a group decide on, overall power resides in the group and not in the rules or the workers. Rules which prove problematic can always be changed.

Recording

Another issue which requires resolution at an early stage, and one which is related to the above discussion, is the question of recording the group sessions. It is not normally appropriate in self-directed action for the workers to make the usual assumption that they will keep their own record of sessions, for their own use and not to be shared with participants. It is more in keeping with the self-directed approach if either the workers maintain a record but share it with group members, in a way that makes it the property of the whole group, or if group members themselves act in this capacity. Members' lack of confidence in writing skills can be tackled by undertaking recording in pairs, for example.

Of course, group recording consists of more than minute taking - at the simplest level an account only of who attended, and the major events and decisions taken at that particular meeting, would entirely omit group process from consideration and would also undersell the detail of the group content. This means that whoever is undertaking the recording, whether worker or member, will need to be helped to learn the skills involved in noting both what the group is doing and what it feels like to be in the group at that time. A useful list of points to look out for in group process is given by Douglas (1976, pp.80-81). Although it is directed at workers, we see no reason why group members should not become skilled in applying it. A model developed in a group of school non-attenders is set out in Figure 2.

Approaching recording in this way means that we would state categorically that it is not appropriate to keep personal files on the members of self-directed groups. The only time when this would happen would be when individual work was being undertaken alongside the groupwork and, in that instance, the file would relate to the latter and not to the member's 'performance' or behaviour in the group.

The uses to which group records may be put obviously include

Figure 2
A Model for Group Recording

Group Issues
What is going on in the group
which is confined to it and not
shared outside - e.g. worker
interventions, young people's
issues, group processes.

Maintaining Contacts
What is shared with other
agencies about the group.
Includes meetings set up to
discuss what is going on and
other feedback.

Workers Issues
How workers operate together.
Resolving differences.

*Interventions Related to Group
Process outside Group Meetings*
Worker attendance at court and
representation in case conferences.
These should be agreed in
consultation with young people.

Future Developments
Discussion of group in terms
of future development. For
example, what impact is the
group having? What needs to
be changed?

from Burley (1982)

---

giving workers and members a concrete reminder of what they have achieved. In addition to this, they are likely to be crucial in assembling any future funding bids for the group when it may be useful to back up statements like 'The group has given talks all over the country' with specific details. Another essential purpose of recording, especially in a field that is still being developed, as this one is, is to provide a basis for written accounts of groupwork activity which may encourage others to take on further work of this kind.

Recording frequently consists of more than a social work-type running-record of the group meetings and of any other meetings or conferences in which the group is involved. We shall see, in Chapter Four, for instance, how flip charts (newsprint sheets) can be preserved from group exercises to serve as an 'art gallery', or group 'memory', and to this we would add further variations, such as a photographic or more elaborate exhibition on a group's work to date, a video, or tape/slide show, or a newspaper cuttings collection if the group has attracted considerable media publicity.

Sometimes such materials are stored and only occasionally referred back to, to boost group morale or remind the members of the goals and tasks they have set themselves. Other groups may routinely use records of the direction they have set and their achievements to date. The flip charts on which issues and plans of action have been brainstormed and analysed, for example, can usefully be retained and regularly displayed at meetings to form the basis of subsequent work. The Ainsley Teenage Action Group always took care to work in this way since they found it empowering to see all their work as a progression towards a clear set of goals. The Nottingham 'Who Cares' Group operated in a similar way by gathering together all its memorabilia into a box which came to every meeting and became the embodiment of where the group had been and what it had done. Another good example of imaginative recording is provided by Croft and Beresford (1987, pp.12-13), in relation to a group of housing estate residents funded by a local Family Services Unit. They kept a scrapbook in which anyone could write down their feelings, experiences and ideas.

Roles in Relationship to Group Membership and Individual Work

Part of the process of negotiating a working agreement with the members of a self-directed group consists of clarifying which matters it is proper to bring to the group and which should be dealt with outside of it. Brown and Caddick (1986, p.101) have questioned how the self-directed approach 'incorporates the agency's goals in relation to individual behaviour', with particular reference to social control functions, and also 'whether there is a place within it for individual members to work at their own . . . personal matters, perhaps of health, role-change or relationship'. Unequivocally, we would answer that a groupworker using the self-directed model would not put any of these matters on the agenda *in the group* . Individual members themselves are, of course, always free to mention in a group meeting that they are due up in court again on Tuesday, or had a flaming row at home again last week, or any other current preoccupation, but this would be because it arose in the course of conversation and not in the expectation that the group would 'down tools' to focus on the matter, as might happen in a group which had a therapeutic purpose. When an individual problem arises spontaneously, it may well be discussed but is often a prelude for either workers or other members to refocus on the goals or tasks in hand. For example, in a group held in a penal setting, a number of people wanted to know about parole or visiting arrangements; answers to specific factual questions on these matters, as well as strong expressions of discontent by particular individuals, led into broader discussions of how to 'play the system' for an early release and of the unfairness of the 'system' overall (Badham, 1989). What is not appropriate at such a time is for the workers to move into an individualised perspective which would be at odds with the overall goals of the group.

This is not to say, however, that individual needs are ignored. On occasion, the same or a different worker does retain a continuing one-to-one casework relationship, sometimes on a statutory basis, with a group member outside of the group. Where this is the case, the worker is able to make it clear to all group members that he or she (or the rest of the team) remains available to offer individual support at times of difficulty. The probation officer who worked with the Ainsley Teenage Action Group left open the offer of individual contact for occasions like this. Some members did indeed ask to see him individually when they felt they needed to do so. As a group develops over time, however, members increasingly offer each other this support both inside and outside the group and, where they feel something to be beyond their scope, will often help the person concerned to seek appropriate sources of help outside the group.

We would not deny that very many group members feel that their personal problems have eased, or that they have become more able or more motivated to tackle them, as a result of their membership of a self-directed group. These benefits we have elsewhere referred to as 'secondary advantages' of membership of self-directed groups (Mullender and Ward, 1985, p.156).

Conclusion

In this chapter we have begun to describe how the achievement of empowerment can be begun through the medium of open planning. What has emerged is that empowering values are demonstrated through a different kind of planning from the traditional, worker-led approach. Recognising that people themselves have skills and abilities (Principle One) and, particularly, that the self-directed model requires people to make decisions for themselves and to take full control of setting the goals for the work (Principle Five), ways have to be found to involve them as fully as possible right from the beginning. The conduct of the group, recording and control of resources are also negotiated by workers and members together. The message to be conveyed is that the group belongs to its members right from the start.

For many erstwhile 'clients', 'patients' or 'pupils', the degree of power they hold and learn to exercise in the group, in conjunction with the other group members, is their first experience of feeling in control of anything in their lives. Often, everything else - including previous professional help - has appeared to happen to them, or to be done to them, without their own volition and without their views on the matter even being sought or noticed to any great extent. Beginning successfully to assume some control, in and through the group, not only changes the way that others regard the group members, as negative labels are challenged, but also fundamentally alters their own perception of themselves. They slowly come to see themselves as people who have rights and they also gradually develop the skills to exercise those rights effectively. This is fundamental to the concept of empowerment.

The next three chapters will show group members continuing to exercise control, initially over setting the agenda for the group and then in taking action on their own behalf.

Chapter Four

The Group Prepares to Take Action

The pre-planning and planning stages of the self-directed model, as presented in Chapters Three and Four, have covered all the preparations for a piece of intervention, including the process of getting the participants together with the workers on the basis of a preliminary working agreement. This led on from the worker team's concern to clarify its own value position and to translate this into practice through planning in partnership with users.

The role of the workers now becomes one of facilitating the participants themselves to move beyond joining the group into planning to take action. This chapter will explore the nature of the techniques and skills which best achieve this, within the framework of Stage 'C' of the model. Although utilised selectively, the techniques we recommend are not peculiar to the self-directed approach. What is different here is that their use is imbued with the underlying values or principles for practice which we set out in Chapter Two, just as was the planning process in Chapter Three.

> It is not so much a matter of adopting new methods but of establishing current methods within a new framework.... There is nothing inherently radical or conservative in any method. It is the purposes of those using them that breathe into them one or other of these characteristics. (Ragg, 1977, p.145)

A Detailed Examination of Stage 'C' of the Model

We will now demonstrate, as was outlined in the framework of the model in Chapter One, that the overall worker responsibility in Stage C is to help members move through the steps of answering the questions 'WHAT', 'WHY' and 'HOW': that is, to assist them in stating their problems (WHAT) and in arriving at their own analysis of those problems by comparing experiences (WHY), prior to deciding for themselves what priorities to set and what action to take (HOW). At all times, the workers are active in creating a favourable environment for this step-by-step development: by maximising participants' autonomy, stimulating their motivation, and in encouraging and supporting their own initiatives.

Let us remind ourselves how Stage C was presented in Chapter One:

Stage C: The Group Prepares to Take Action

The group is helped to explore the questions
WHAT?, WHY? and HOW?

Step 5: The workers facilitate the group setting its own agenda of issues:
ASKING THE QUESTION - WHAT are the problems to be tackled?

Step 6: The workers help the group to analyse the wider causes of these problems:
ASKING THE QUESTION - WHY do the problems exist?

Step 7: The workers enable the group to decide what action needs to be taken, set priorities and allocate tasks:
ASKING THE QUESTION - HOW can we produce change?

In this stage, therefore, there is a critical movement from exploration, through understanding, to action. All three steps or phases are equally important but we tend to place a special emphasis on the middle one - step 6, or the 'WHY?' phase - simply because it is so often neglected by other authors and practitioners. They often neglect to ask the question 'WHY' themselves and almost never encourage service users to ask it. In order to emphasise its key place in self-directed work, the more complex understanding - which the 'WHY' question is intended to strive towards - is incorporated as a basic principle of the approach, expressed as Principle 3:

> The problems that service users face are complex and responses to them need to reflect this. People's problems can never be fully understood if they are seen solely as a result of personal inadequacies. Issues of oppression, social policy, the environment and the economy are, more often than not, and particularly in the lives of service users, major contributory forces. *Practice should reflect this understanding.*

This principle sums up the dangers inherent in moving too rapidly from considering 'WHAT' is wrong to deciding 'HOW' to take action to put it right, without pausing to ask 'WHY' it was wrong in the first place. Such an over-hasty assessment leads to the assumption that personal inadequacies can be treated as the root cause of most human suffering because it glosses over underlying social factors. There needs to be a vital middle stage which consists of service users reflecting on, and coming to an understanding in social structural terms of 'WHY' they face the problems which exist in their lives.

Without this crucial 'WHY' stage, the question 'HOW' leads to some extremely misleading answers. Participants in self-directed action could, for example, jump straight from the decision that 'WHAT' is wrong is high unemployment to the view that 'HOW' best to tackle it would be to 'repatriate all the blacks', if they did not stop to understand that the national and international economic and social forces which create unemployment are far wider than either the white or the black working class. It is not necessary to become experts on the workings of high finance; only to see that it may suit certain interests very well to have white and black scrapping amongst themselves over who gets the few jobs at the local factory instead of lobbying for the economic regeneration of the entire area. Similarly, turning to a group of young offenders where 'WHAT' troubles them most is police harassment, the expected message from the authorities is that keeping their heads down and their noses clean constitutes 'HOW' to rectify the problem. Yet the example of the Ainsley Teenage Action Group, given in the next chapter, shows that an entirely different solution is possible.

We recognise that, without the question 'WHY?' - and without the value-base to which it closely relates - it would actually be dangerous to offer workers the more effective and more confident approach to practice which the model implies. If this were utilised to arrive at misleading answers, as demonstrated above, its impact would be more damaging than merely allowing present ways of working to continue undisturbed. The techniques and the values within the model must always, therefore, be taken together as a package and not disaggregated.

A New Respect and Other Benefits for Service Users

It is only the full and detailed consideration of 'WHY' problems have actually come about - which may take weeks, months, or even years - which will prevent people from selling themselves or other oppressed people short when it comes to taking appropriate action. The workers' role in all this is to facilitate their delving deeper and deeper into the causes which underlie difficulties. Workers are likely to learn a good deal themselves in the process, including that they should never underestimate the potential understanding of those with whom they work.

It is not only the 'WHY' stage which gives workers a new insight into the hidden strengths of service users (see Principle 1). During the initial 'WHAT' stage, participants have the shock of being asked, often for the first time, what they see as their own problems and they rise readily to the challenge. Giving them a voice (see Principle 2) and a combined confidence (Principle 4) frequently opens the flood-gates on pent-up resentments but it also reveals the most astonishing frankness of expression and resilience against repeated disaster and in the face of unremitting humiliation by the authorities. This stage is both humbling and uplifting. It gives one both joy and shame in shared humanity.

The 'HOW' stage, too, during which there is a detailed consideration of all the various remedies to try and apply to the situation, aims to give people a sense of their own positive qualities and abilities, through discovering new responses to situations and developing the skills to deal with them. Instead of being content with everybody else 'blaming the victim', i.e. themselves, this takes service users into the realm of social issues and opens up new and unanticipated options for action in the public sphere. A spin-off of taking the pressure of blame off the individuals concerned and offering them the chance to take action for themselves is usually a marked improvement in their personal esteem. Participants gain still more because they value their own efforts, not just in terms of improved knowledge and skills, but also in terms of their activities having very practical benefits for themselves.

What we propose to do for the remainder of this chapter is to look in greater detail at the various elements of Stage C: asking the questions WHAT, WHY and HOW, and in preparation for TAKING ACTION on the issues that emerge. We will examine how these steps might appear in practice and go on to consider some of the questions that arise. We will be drawing attention to a number of techniques and exercises which can be used in non-oppressive ways (Principle 5). We are not attempting to present a comprehensive list but will be outlining those which we have found to be effective in our own practice, or in that described to us by practitioner colleagues. It is notoriously difficult to acknowledge sources for any particular techniques which may now be presented in greatly modified form from the one invented. However, where possible, we will attempt to identify sources, which will lead readers naturally towards developing their own repertoire. Collections which we have turned to repeatedly are those found in ACW (1981), Hope and Timmel (1984), Jelfs (1982) and Taylor and Kemp (undated).

Asking the Question WHAT

The first area of activity, once the initial working agreement has been reached between workers and participants (the point we reached at the end of Chapter Three), is for the group to begin its search for collectively agreed goals. The workers' first priority is for ways of working which will help service users to express all the concerns which are uppermost in their lives so that they can go on to set their own agenda of issues. This is what we refer to as 'asking the question WHAT?'

Techniques Used to Elicit, Discuss and 'Own' Participants' Views

BRAINSTORMING

A classic technique in self-directed groups - particularly at this early stage of needing to encourage the free expression of considerable pent-up resentment and hitherto unvoiced views, is that of 'brainstorming'. Most people are now very familiar with brainstorming as a way of working both in practice and in education; it consists of posing a straightforward question or topic to the group and simply recording all the responses which are forthcoming so that everyone present can see what is being written. There is no discussion of the ideas as they are recorded; members simply state or shout out their own immediate reactions, for a set period of time or until they are exhausted, and are discouraged from reacting to other people's at this stage.

The second stage of the exercise is to discuss all the points which members have listed in a search for linking themes and common threads, so that what at first looks like a completely chaotic jumble begins to take on a definable shape. Again, group members are encouraged to express and compare their own ideas, opinions and experiences; these are not filtered out by the workers on the basis of age, status, or loudness, for example.

The skills required by the workers at both stages of a brainstorming exercise include those of eliciting comments, recording them accurately but succinctly, and 'spotting' what is only hesitantly forthcoming - here it is useful for one or more of the workers to sit amongst the group and to pick up any 'mutterings' so as to be able to draw out the contributions and encourage the most reticent to participate. As groups develop, participants themselves will be able to act in the recorder or 'rapporteur' role, and some will be able to do this straight away. The other roles, too, may be taken by group members where appropriate, but usually at the expense of that person's contribution to the ideas which are forthcoming.

Typically, both recording of ideas and sorting them into groupings is done on flip charts, or on a larger blackboard if one is available - though the latter is often less desirable because the record is not permanent unless it is laboriously copied out again afterwards. Copier-boards (white-boards with built-in photocopiers), where available, combine the advantages of both. More imaginatively, as was mentioned in Chapter Three, we have come across the brainstorming technique being used in a totally impromptu way with a natural group of young people on a street corner by a detached youth worker. He conveniently carried round a piece of chalk in his pocket and simply wrote down what they said were the problems facing them on their estate on the paving slabs in front of them. All discussion exercises should ideally be recorded in some way so that the material they produce will be available to the group whenever it is needed. Readers are not advised to carry paving slabs home with them, however!

There are other reasons why brainstorming is a very useful technique at the earliest stages of a group. Individual members are not in undue focus and thus it helps them come to feel at home in the group and has the effect of drawing people together. A number of conditions have been found to assist this to happen:

- suspended judgement on ideas proferred, with no criticism;
- freewheeling, with no limit on the type of ideas - in fact, often the 'strangest' ones can lead the group in new and rewarding directions;
- as many ideas as possible, the more the better;
- cross-fertilisation, through ideas being combined and improved in the second stage of the brainstorm.

A simple framework for forward planning can be introduced into brainstorming on the basis of 'likes'/'dislikes'. This was done with the Ainsley Group of young people. The workers put a sheet of paper on the wall of the school dining-hall where the group members had negotiated a venue for their initial meeting. After discussion over refreshments the workers wrote two headings, 'good things' and 'bad things' on the estate. This prompted talk about what there was to do locally and about group members themselves. Ideas did not flow quickly to start with but, with prompting, a list emerged:

BAD	GOOD
Nothing to do	Swimming Baths
Boredom	Chippy
Schools	Laughs with mates
Police	
No open space to use	
Lack of respect	
Banned from baths	

The young people then came up with several ideas on how to improve such things as facilities, lack of respect and the swimming baths ban. There and then, they decided to meet weekly to plan a campaign for their own youth club. Their immediate request was for a meeting-place of their own - off the streets - where they could play games, listen to music, drink coffee and generally attempt to avoid conflict with adults which, in their view, had created trouble, offences and court appearances in the past. For the next week they all planned to walk round the estate to look at the facilities and places mentioned. The organisation of topics from a brainstorm into 'good' and 'bad' lists can also provide a perfect basis for a force-field analysis (see later in chapter).

Perhaps no other exercise can occupy quite the place in self-directed work that is accorded to brainstorming - with its opportunities for all group members to participate and its drawing out of so many spontaneous but normally unspoken feelings and views (see Principle 2) - but there are certainly many other techniques which are employed.

ART GALLERY

Where flip charts are used, they invariably become key working tools in later sessions of the group so they should never be lightly discarded. In the early days, it is often useful to display them on the walls of the group's meeting-room at the start of every session. In the short term, this provides concrete illustrative material to remind everyone what the group is working on; that is, its answers so far to the question 'WHAT?' Having this visual record enlivens and speeds up the discussion by allowing the group to capitalise on, and to take responsibility for work achieved so far.

In the longer term, as all working charts are preserved, they are recognised as the common property of the group, binding people together through an open, visual history of a campaign; this gives group members a sense of movement to their work and also provides a symbolic focal point with which members can identify. As time goes on, it may become a routine event at the start of every meeting for the members themselves to put up the 'art gallery' of flip charts on the wall; like the family portraits of the nobility, they become the group's heritage - a focus for group identity, cohesion, and continuity. Crucially, they are also available as a foundation for moving the group on beyond the 'WHAT?' stage into asking the questions "WHY' do these problems confront us, and 'HOW' do we intend to tackle them?

FILMS AND VIDEOS

It is often possible to initiate fruitful discussion in a group by showing pre-recorded video or film material that focuses on similar social problems to those which confront the members themselves. Either documentaries or fictional works with a heavy social content may be used. Provided that due attention is paid to the legal position on copyright, material which has been commercially produced for television may be particularly good because it is usually digestible, highly visual, and may already be familiar from members' own viewing. As well as the obvious documentaries, even material from chat-shows and 'soaps' can be used if it comments on a relevant issue such as the position of women (How did this female celebrity make it to the top? Were obstacles placed in her way?) or a topical social issue. Media representation of black people, for example, may be more clearly seen in popular than in 'worthy' programmes.

The disadvantage of pre-recorded material is that there is never a complete fit between what is seen on the screen and service users' own lived experience. It can only ever constitute a 'jumping off' point. In addition, the potential themes for discussion may crowd in upon one another so that it is hard to retain them all in mind until the end of the programme. Unless one is prepared to make liberal use of the pause or freeze-frame button - which has its own disadvantages of discontinuity and possible annoyance - much of the detailed value of the film's content may be lost. This factor can be exacerbated by the habits of superficial and interrupted viewing which tend to have built up around television; it may not draw out people's most discriminating reactions and it may encourage the kind of passivity and even torpor which are very difficult to shake in any ensuing discussion. On the other hand, seeing a familiar programme in the unfamiliar setting of the group may inject it with sufficient 'surprise' element to awaken renewed interest, whilst retaining feelings of 'safety' and of everyday relevance in relation to content. The programme could, perhaps, be shown twice: once all through over coffee, and a second time, with pauses, when the group is in session and can discuss what emerges from it.

STATEMENT CARDS

An easy and enjoyable exercise which brings out a richness of material for discussion involves the use of index cards. Statements are written on these by the group members (with assistance if writing is a problem). Group members each write down their own ideas - for example on what they see the chief problems facing them to be - one idea on each of five index cards. These are then pooled, shuffled and laid out face-upwards in a big space on the floor, or on a large table. Members are asked to read them and to take out three cards, other than their own, expressing ideas with which they agree.

The whole group is then asked to find common themes amongst the cards they have chosen, initially by finding someone else who has a card similar to one of their's and laying both together on the table. Other people can then add cards which match the emerging topics. Discussion opens up across the group around themes which do and don't link up, and around similar and opposing selections of cards. The cards which were not taken up can be drawn into this - and in practice usually find a place on one of the piles which have been formed.

The workers may or may not need to help participants to go and ask what cards other people have drawn and to spot common themes until they get the idea for themselves. The workers also need to concentrate on noticing, and where appropriate highlighting to the whole group, issues both of content and of process. Content issues include those points on which all or most people agree, and those on which there is the most dissension. From this, members can identify shared interests and matters on which it is possible to move forward straight away. This is particularly useful where a group has previously been bogged down in disagreement over petty detail, and has been oblivious to whole other areas of agreement. Group process issues include members' ability to consult one another increasingly freely as the exercise progresses, to 'hear' the various angles on an argument more effectively, and to enjoy the feeling of the whole group beginning to gel together.

The exercise does demand that members should be able to read and have some rudimentary writing skills, as well as being reasonably articulate and able to listen. It is, of course, useful in helping them to develop the skills of offering their own views and listening to one another. In another, more complex variation of the game, the cards are not laid out but are dealt, face down, to the players with a central pile left over, also placed face down. Players then have to decide which of the cards they have been dealt they happen to agree with and which they want to exchange. This involves making quite fine distinctions as to the acceptability of a particular way of phrasing one's own views and assessing whether what one holds in the hand is 'near enough' or should be risked for something still closer. The parallels with real life negotiating skills are obvious.

Although this exercise has been described as playing a game and is fun, it is not only suitable for young people's groups and it does have a serious purpose. Adult groups, too, can find it extremely useful to move away from pure discussion into activities which are fun but which sharpen the clarity of the debate. It is important that all groups, of whatever age, should be enjoyable to belong to as well as having a more serious side. We have used the technique frequently, in consultancies and training events as well as in group and project work, and have frequently wished we had a camera to record their enthusiasm as they crawl around the floor making elaborate arrangments of cards. These can, incidentally, be sticky-taped together in their rows and afterwards displayed on the wall. Better still, they can be arranged in the first place on a large sheet of paper and secured in place when everyone is satisfied with their eventual positions.

The statement-card exercise can also be used in the HOW stage of a group for focusing on what different participants want to do about an issue.

Concluding Comments on Exercises in This Section

Inevitably these exercises do not reflect the full range of possibilities for asking the question WHAT. However, they are ones which we ourselves and close colleagues have come to use again and again. In talking to other practitioners who have sought to develop groups which empower their users, we have found expressions of frustration that the standard 'games' texts provide little for the early stages of a group beyond 'ice-breaking' and 'group-building' exercises. These are often based around constructed, fantasy or even fairy-tale scenarios; they decontextualise practice from service users' real world and thereby establish the workers too strongly as directors of the activities, the tone and the agenda in the group.

The exercises we have described are of proven effectiveness both in breaking the ice and in building the group. Yet they do this through focusing on participants' lived experience. They get straight to the heart of what most concerns group members and, consequently, keep the emphasis on their words, their priorities and their choices. The workers are facilitators and enablers of the activities and the discussion. They do not impose their own topics or insert their own ideas. Every single group member is involved and the workers' skill can be used in drawing everyone in: ensuring that quieter members, such as women or girls in mixed groups, someone who stammers or who mentions the things others would like to ignore, are not overlooked or rejected by the rest of the group. The workers also need to select exercises which match the abilities of the group, without underestimating these, and which catch their interest.

Asking the Question WHY

As was pointed out earlier in this chapter, working with group members to analyse WHY the issues they have identified exist is the distinctive feature of practice which seeks to achieve empowerment. Without it, there can be no awareness of wider-scale oppression, no moving beyond blaming oneself for one's problems into greater awareness and the pursuit of social change. To jump straight from identifying WHAT is wrong into the practicalities (the HOW) of achieving change would be to collude with a process in which explanations of the responsibility for problems are usually sought in the private world around individual and family, either because this is the extent of the worker's own understanding or because it appears to them to make intervention more feasible. To ask the question 'WHY?' brings social issues into play and opens up new options for action in the public world. It represents the application of the values of empowerment (see Chapters One and Two) in practice.

Techniques Used to Ask the Question WHY

Whether, and how, the question WHY is asked has its roots in the way workers frame their questions and responses during the WHAT phase - as well as in the ways they carry these forward into the kind of discussion which will be outlined in this section. How such framing takes place depends on the assumptions and values that workers bring to their work. It is for this reason that the exploration of workers' own values was stressed as an inescapable aspect of the first stage of the model. It remains so here. For example, asking the question WHY puts oppression firmly on the agenda and requires that special and subtle attention be paid to Principle 5; as Woodrow and Terry (1979) put it, 'Working for social change means systematically dismantling [the] interlocking systems of oppression.'

We will now move on to looking at some particular techniques which help to raise the question WHY and which can encourage a generally anti-oppressive view.

CONSCIOUSNESS RAISING

One of the most clearly appropriate techniques to use in empowering groups, and one which tends to lead automatically from WHAT into WHY (though it is less good at tackling HOW: Freeman, 1970, p.5) is consciousness raising - argued in our opening chapter to be a key aspect of empowerment. In novel form, Shulman (1979, pp.228-229) describes the roots of the basic technique as derived from the exercise of 'speaking bitterness' in revolutionary China: 'The peasants were able to change their lives by examining their own personal everyday experience of oppression. They got a lot of strength from talking about it and comparing stories.'

In the early women's consciousness raising groups, participants would sit in a circle and speak in turn about the everyday circumstances and events of their lives. No one remained silent; no one interrupted or passed comment. This made it possible to share things which would have seemed inconsequential or wrong-headed in other, notably male, company. Women slowly learned to recognise and to value their own and each other's experiences (Principle 1) and, in turn, to voice these more freely (Principle 2). Gradually, it emerged that women had in common the same feelings of drudgery, duty, guilt, inadequacy and anger at housework, sole responsibility for child-rearing, and being taken for granted or abused by men. Issues that individuals had not previously even recognised as such - like who performed basic chores in the home, or how men assumed women to be stupid and unreliable - were heard repeatedly until the conclusion became inescapable that they affected all women, from all backgrounds, *and could not be attributable any longer to individual failings on the part of those women.* It was the fundamental relationships between men and women, and women's own valuation of themselves, which needed to change.

Just as the women's movement reframed what really mattered to women under the phrase 'the personal is political', so the raised awareness of the Black consciousness movement confronted and reversed the negative valuation of dominant white society through the slogan 'Black is beautiful'. The Black and In Care Group's newsletter takes this motto as its title and, taking the February 1990 issue as an example, links broader international awareness of black oppression (the release of Nelson Mandela) with the need for a detailed analysis of the way black children are treated in the white care system: whether ethnic food is cooked, whether black history and culture are celebrated, whether racist language is outlawed, and whether same race placements are sought.

Webb (1985, pp.97-98) sums up how consciousness raising works towards illuminating present understanding and showing it to reflect only partial truth. Through pooling and exploring what participants know at first hand as their own life experience, movement towards what the truth actually is - the WHY - is achieved: 'new knowing emerges from within the old as this becomes progressively more bankrupt in its capacity to deal with lived reality' (ibid, p.98). On this basis, effective action can be built.

An Example

The Braunstone Women's Self-Help and Action Group went through all these stages. It was started by two social workers who were keen to work with women members in their own right as women, rather than through their relationship to the department as mothers, carers and clients - filed as 'child care' cases. Their previous social workers had sought the women out individually to discuss all the things that seemed to go wrong in daily life (Lane, 1986, p.112) which tended to make them feel responsible, guilty, failures (Donnelly, 1986, pp.12 and 18) despite the fact that they were shouldering 'an intolerable burden' (Hale, 1983, p.169). At first, the women attending the group simply talked about themselves and their experiences. It was not long before 'we were surprised to find other people had the same problems' (this and other direct quotes are from Mullender, unpublished account, unless otherwise indicated). Realising that the company of other women could be uplifting, they built new friendship and support networks through the group which, as well as relieving isolation, fostered self-confidence, self-esteem and self-awareness.

As they began to see that other women had the same kinds of problems and obstacles to their development as they did, they gradually began to recognise the general social oppression of all women and their own potential power and ability to gain control over their lives. They found this whole process of achieving new forms of understanding a revelation. As Lorna put it: 'It's just amazing that someone else is saying the same as happened to you - it's a really unbelievable experience and instantly brings you out of yourself.' Another is quoted as saying: 'You know that you're no longer on your own, that others feel the same way - that you're not mad, or, if you are, so is everyone' (Wright, 1985, p.82). To take just one example, after sharing the pain and degradation of account after account of severe domestic violence which relatives, friends and often social workers had told each woman she 'must have provoked', the realisation now dawned on them that 'If you, you and you are battered, it can't be your faults'. After a time, then, the women began to see that problems so common and widespread must have wider causes. The explanation of domestic violence begins to move away from one which 'blames the victim' (Ryan, 1971) to one which identifies a wider system of oppression of women by men in our society. Campbell (1984, p.93) is clear that:

domestic violence . . . is something men do to women, not because they're mad or homicidal maniacs, but as an expression of ordinary domestic conflict between unequals. The violence is only the exercise of an ultimate weapon available to men.

Longres and McLeod (1980, p.275) summarise, from their own experience in groupwork, the three stages of consciousness raising through which this recognition, or movement from WHAT to WHY happens:

themes generally surfaced as a private trouble experienced by an individual participant. As the discussions proceeded, however, attention shifted to the related experiences of others in the group, and then to the analysis of the structural sources of the shared troubles.

The same authors (Longres and McLeod, 1980, p.268), influenced by Freire (1972), are clear that consciousness raising must go beyond increased understanding into action: 'reflection in search of understanding dehumanizing social structures . . . . [and] . . . action aimed at altering societal conditions. The two must go hand in hand; action without reflection is as unjustifiable as reflection without action.' In the North Braunstone group, reflection led to action both at the individual level, through an increasing ability to be assertive - Di began to expect her partner to take his turn at looking after the kids, while Janet found the confidence to throw hers out, telling him to 'go and live with his fancy woman' - and at the wider level, with the women taking part in campaigns and conferences and eventually establishing their own women's centre.

THE WORKERS' ROLE: MOVING ON TO 'PROBLEM-POSING'
In practice, for the workers, to achieve this kind of success means basing their style of intervention firmly on Principle 1: recognising that members already have 'skills, understanding and ability', the workers need to develop a non-patronising approach based on the belief that people already know and understand many of the issues surrounding the reality of their lives (Longres and McLeod, 1980, p.269). They also need techniques for encouraging groups to ask themselves the broader questions. Provided they can do this, they do have a particular contribution to make:

> Workers do have a certain knowledge and expertise that derives from their own experience - from training and from their involvement in practice. This expertise will be largely demonstrated in their ability to develop discussion and to be used as a source of information. It is not an expertise that requires deference from the group, but it is the special contribution made by the social worker. (ibid., p.270)

Specifically, the workers' role is to see that topics come from the group and are kept in play long enough for broader understanding to develop. Just as the brainstorms and other exercises asking the question WHAT, had this purpose, so the ideas which were forthcoming then should now be handed back to the group in a *problem-posing* way (Freire, 1972), in order for the group to gain more awareness of the total issue. Hope and Timmel (1984, p.60) summarise the prompts for the ensuing discussion as a series of questions which we have adapted slightly for our own work:

a. Description - *What do you see happening?*
b. Analysis - *Why is it happening?*
c. Related problems - *What problems does it lead to?*
d. Root Causes - *What are the root causes of these problems?*
e. Action planning - *What can we do about it?*

Fritze (1982, p.14), writing about her consciousness raising work with a group of housewives, also describes this as involving a series of questions to be posed by the worker and considered by participants. Hers may be listed thus:

• Who am I?
  How do I feel about it?
  What does that have to do with myself as a woman, and with the position of women in general?
• Where are decisions being taken and how do I as a woman have some control of this?
  How am I influenced, how can I change it and where do I already have some control?

The role which all this indicates for workers is one of fostering and building up a 'dialogue' (Freire, 1972): a process of mutual learning among and with group members. This means threading a way through the maze of information, experience and feelings which *all* participants bring, in order to find broad themes and to keep the flow of discussion and action going (Lovett, 1983, p.82). Hope and Timmell (1984, pp.11 and 60) illustrate this in the following way:

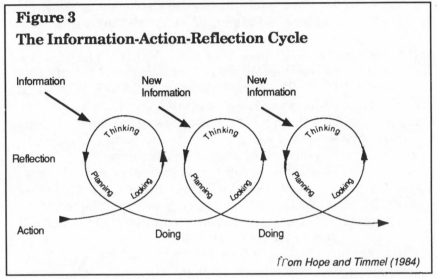

Figure 3

The Information-Action-Reflection Cycle

from Hope and Timmel (1984)

AH-HAH! SEMINARS

A full-scale technique for problem-posing, or asking the question WHY, is that of the Ah-Hah! seminar (GATT-Fly, 1983. N.B: GATT-Fly is a project established in 1973 by Canadian churches across five Christian denominations to work with popular groups, including native people's organisations, for global economic justice). This 'popular education' methodology involves asking participants to create a pictorial representation of their world, showing the inter-relationships of the different features in it, so that they understand clearly for the first time what they knew before in only a partial or confused way (hence the title). Those present sit in a semi-circle round a large sheet of paper, with coloured felt pens available to draw symbols representing various aspects of their lives and the life of their community. Participants can ask one another questions about their drawings and the facilitator also prompts people to think about different parts of their lives and how they fit together, as well as valuing contributions as they are added. In particular, participants may need encouraging to do the first drawings. These should start with a symbol central to the particular group or the reason for holding the seminar: for example, a women's group put a feminist activist at the heart of its drawing while a group of native Americans discussing day care put their children. Although the facilitator can also join in, he or she should not start the drawing off since this can hold others back.

It also helps if earlier work in the group has included drawing. Nothing elaborate is needed; stick people are perfectly adequate, especially as the drawings are discussed as the work goes along.

People should be asked to name the symbols they are drawing and to explain their signifance. The facilitator should ensure that plenty of time is taken over this. Probing questions are asked about each element of the picture: 'What is she doing, this feminist activist? Whose interests does she serve? Who needs her? What problems does she address? What are the factors influencing this situation? What else is going on? How are these factors connected to each other?' (Adams, undated, p.5). In particular, the political, economic and social forces should be analysed in detail: 'Who benefits from the status quo, who loses out, and in what ways? How do all these things link up?' On this analysis, more effective action for change will later be based.

The result of the exercise is that people are enabled to build a picture of the wider social system, on a local, national or international scale, focused around their own place in it. They can then discuss how it is maintained in this form, what needs to change (all marked in one colour), and what can be done to achieve this. The strengths of the model are its simplicity as a technique, the complexity and inter-relatedness of the resulting analysis, the graphic and comprehensible form in which this emerges, the affirmation that groups can conduct their own structural analysis, and the added benefits of developing group control over process and offering an entertaining and creative way of learning.

Like our own work, this technique offers an appropriately empowering methodology for an empowering message and does so by starting from participants' own experiences. It is co-operative and hence helps people to arrive at a collective analysis of their own situation. There is often a low point during the session (which ideally requires a day or two to do properly) when participants see how many powerful forces they have portrayed, all of which are ranged against them (Adams, undated, p.3). With facilitation, however, this can also be the turning-point, before the second half of the discussion time turns towards making plans for action (asking the question HOW). The facilitator should try to ensure that resources and strengths have been included in the picture before this stage in addition to all the problems: features such as networks, friends, allies, people's own strengths and motivations, past successes of the group, other individuals and groups affected by the same negative social forces, and so on, can all be called on when it comes to planning how to fight back. The facilitator needs group process skills, perhaps shared with the group, not only to read the overall emotional climate, but also to encourage the group to look at any blocks which occur and to deal with apparently contradictory views

Debra Lewis and her colleague Marcy Cohen developed a version of the Ah-Hah! technique to use as a full-day workshop at a women's conference. It had to be 'consistent with the feminist principles that the personal is political, and that women's perspective should be central to our work for social change' (Lewis, 1988, p.1). They started from women's family and home lives, then drew in work, community, and the work of women's groups in the region. The wall-sized 'maps' of women's lives which resulted were a graphic representation of the complexity of women's experience. Later, the participants 'analyzed the results by looking for the connections between our lives and the social and political institutions that shape much of our experience. We asked who has control over the problems women face, and who benefits. Finally, we asked ourselves what changes would result in real improvements in our lives' (ibid.). Examples of answers to this last question were: flexible childcare arrangements and work schedules, services planned and controlled by the communities they serve, equality of access to education and expansion of job training for women, and events which are made accessible to isolated, low income, disabled, black and native American women. They found the AH-HAH! concept to be an empowering technique which, because it pushes participants towards seeking their own solutions, has the advantage of offering a natural progression into continuing work. In this way, it leads directly from WHY into HOW.

GATT-Fly's own staff travel the world encouraging the people of developing countries to apply their ability to reach 'a very sophisticated analysis of their situation . . . if given a tool such as the Ah-hah seminar, workers and peasants can be even clearer and sharper in their analysis than the intellectuals' (Howlett, 1985, p.2). This follows an example of a woman rubber plantation worker in Malaysia who recognised the links between her own situation and that of electronics workers in her country who needed to become unionised. Howlett also quotes the words of a participant at a seminar in Thailand:

> The idea of the Ah-hah technique acknowledges dignity, self-discovery and awareness. It is a means to participation and

an education process which leads to action. There is no planned owner of the seminar whose philosophy we are asked to approve of. With the drawing technique we can bring the whole world in front of the participants. They feel they are active, rather than responsive. As a result, they realize their power that they can make the whole world [sic]; they can dictate to the world; and they realize what potential they have.'

Asking the question 'WHY?' is intended to help group participants feel for themselves that oppressed people are only oppressed because (and for as long as) they do not perceive their common interests or recognise their collective strength. All the exercises in this section are designed to overcome such obstacles to action and the pursuit of change.

A Concluding Example of Asking the Question WHY

Introducing the question WHY, though the answers may not always extend to global understanding, does consistently widen the areas of concern and potential action that users will identify and hence makes a major difference to the work of every ordinary professional worker. It will extend to external forces their view of the relevant and the possible. The way this can unfold, moving out from personal problems to give access to public issues - provided the worker facilitates rather than blocks it - can be encapsulated in a practice example concerning a group for parents of children with learning difficulties:

> [The group], which had been started by one hospital social worker with the intention of helping the parents to come to terms with their feelings of loss, anger and grief at having had a handicapped child, was taken over by a second worker who as well as valuing those aspects of the work, gave the members more opportunity to voice their own grievances. She did not use selective rewarding (approving nods, smiles and 'mms' at the appropriate points) to direct them back to their emotional reactions once their initial 'coming to terms' had occurred, but allowed their opinions on a range of issues to emerge by asking open-ended questions such as 'What is the worst thing now?' and 'Why is it like it is?' Gradually, the parents turned of their own accord to issues about lack of resources, and the way they had been treated. They have subsequently put pressure on the NHS locally to provide more short-term care

beds, and they have also gingered up the local MENCAP group by involving it, too, in campaigning to change those medical practices, NHS policies, or gaps in resources, which led to the births of some of their brain-damaged children in the first place. (Mullender and Ward, 1985, p.157)

Establishing Priorities: Moving to the Question HOW

Addressing the question WHY has been directed towards opening out options for action by enabling group members to reach a broader social understanding. The question now arises of where attention should be focused, given the range of possibilities this broader vision will have brought into the group's ambit. They will need to set priorities, strategies, tactics and tasks.

Feasibility Exercises

Following the process of identification (WHAT) and analysis (WHY) of issues which the group wants to work on, then, feasibility exercises can be used to plan the specific action the group can undertake. Thus, the question HOW is asked by breaking down the issues into component parts which are comprehensible and manageable, and which can then be allocated as specific tasks.

GRIDS

The various elements of an issue taken from a brainstorm flip chart or off index cards, for example (see earlier in the chapter: asking the question WHAT), can be plotted onto a grid in order to identify short-term, medium-term and longer-term tasks, and whether additional help will be required to meet them:

Figure 4

	Now	Soon	Later
By us			
With help			
By others			

Other decisions facing the group can be plotted in a similar way, for example onto a 'resources grid' where the specifics of resources the group will need rather than tasks to be preformed are explored.

BULL'S EYE EXERCISE.

A similar effect can be achieved using concentric circles, in an exercise described by Taylor and Kemp (undated):

Figure 5

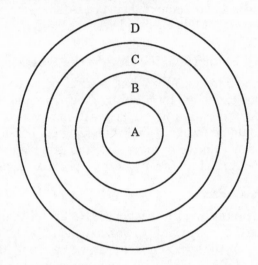

Circle A represents situations that can be changed completely by members;
Circle B represents situations that members can change with help;
Circle C represents situations that members cannot change, but where they can
    influence others to do so;
Circle D represents situations outside the influence of members.

from Taylor and Kemp (undated)

Additional Comment on the Preceding Exercises

In the course of one or both of these exercises and the discussion they generate, an *action plan* will have begun to be self-evident. It will consist of a balance of short- and long-term goals, individual tasks and collective action, self-help and areas in which it will be necessary to influence other people. The grid or circle can provide a useful initial means of setting this out. The grid, however, has the additional advantage of not implying that change will come about through some kind of linear progression but shows that it will be affected by forces operating at various levels. It also shows how the course of change, or the outcome of action, cannot be neatly predicted.

FORCE-FIELD ANALYSIS

Given these complexities, this exercise (Jelfs, 1982, p. 60) becomes useful in concentrating on the development of action once a specific goal for change has been located. (See Figure 6.)

It represents the fact that situations, even the status quo, always involve dynamic forces. To develop the 'force-field analysis', the group writes the goal at the top of a flip chart. The top of the paper is then treated as the goal and the bottom as the opposite, or least desired outcome. A horizontal line is drawn across the middle. In the bottom half of the sheet, the positive forces - those assisting change and working *towards* the sought-for goal - can be plotted with arrows pointing up towards it. In the top half, are placed the negative forces, resisting change, with arrows pointing downwards. The more sophisticated artists may wish to make the arrows of varying lengths and thicknesses, or of different colours, to show that some forces for or against change have greater or lesser longevity or strength. The balance of the arrows/forces overall explains why the status quo, represented by the mid-way line, is currently held where it is. Strengthening the forces pushing up to the goal, or weakening those opposing this momentum, would push the line closer to the goal.

The key to the value of the exercise is that, from the force-field pattern, one can identify three possible ways forward: to strengthen the forces for change, to weaken the restraining or

Figure 6
Force Field Analysis

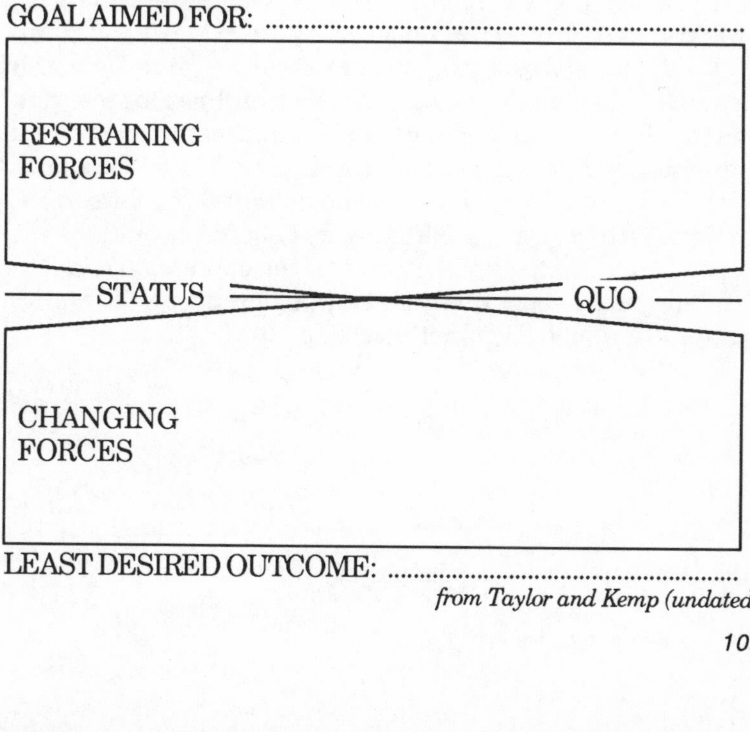

GOAL AIMED FOR: ....

RESTRAINING
FORCES

——— STATUS ═══════════ QUO ———

CHANGING
FORCES

LEAST DESIRED OUTCOME: ....

from Taylor and Kemp (undated)

opposing forces, or to do both. In most practice only the first is actively considered as workers push stubbornly towards what they want to see happen, with the sole exception of trying to talk others round to their own point of view. The force-field exercise opens up more options and also makes it possible to consider whether strong or rapid movement in one direction will cause a backlash in the other. How fragile is the current status quo? Possible actions in each of the three categories can be listed by brainstorming. They can also be considered in the light of further questions such as:

- What is it feasible for us to do as things stand?
- Which opposing forces are weakest and easiest to tackle?
- Which potential alliances are strongest?
- What are others doing?
- Can both positive and negative forces be tackled at the same time?

Clearly there is potential for organising on a grid the information and ideas thus acquired.

Conclusion: Keeping the Values in Play

Presented in these terms - in the form of exercises which we have found useful in groups to ask the questions WHAT, WHY, and HOW - Stage C of the model might appear rather mechanistic. However, as options for action emerge in response to the question HOW, it remains essential to challenge the group to consider these in the light of the overall values we outlined for the work in Chapter Two. This includes the commitment to confronting oppression and is achieved by continuing to ask the question WHY. The result will be that some potential answers to HOW are favoured over others. Thus, we do not accept solutions which empower one group at the expense of the oppression of another, as is alleged in some community work practice with working-class white people (Dominelli, 1988, p.16).

Chapter Five

Taking Action

A Detailed Examination of Stage 'D' of the Model

Once priorities have been established by asking and answering the questions WHAT, WHY and HOW, the task is for group members to apply their knowledge and skills collectively to action, still on the basis of the underlying principles of the model and of the analysis they arrived at in answering the question WHY.

For many groups, this will mean mounting a major public campaign. Others become involved in a long-term series of campaigns focused around one central issue, such as disability or the needs of a local black community. Still others, such as Nottingham Advocacy Group, exist more to create representative forums and services which may, in turn, become the seat of particular campaigns as they become more established and vocal. The common philosophy which all such groups share is nicely illustrated by the fact that the parent of a member of one of the earliest young people's social action groups, whose awareness of the overall approach was raised through her and her son's involvement, is now employed in the mental health field as a paid worker with Nottingham Advocacy Group. This also indicates how far people can progress as a result of self-directed groups and campaigns.

In the outline of the model in Chapter One, we pointed out that steps 5 to 8 may recur several times, in other words, more than one round of action may well be needed before the goal is achieved. Each time, the broad tasks which a campaigning group undertakes tend to cover: collecting the information to make their case, mobilising the support of local residents and of the local authority, heightening the visibility of the issue they are fighting for through use of the media and inviting key personnel from public bodies to meet them, and raising enough funds to run the group and the campaign. Responsibilities for all this work have to be assigned, as well as for additional tasks which arise periodically, such as running public meetings. In such cases, community work, with its emphasis on collective ways of working, offers a range of appropriate, practical approaches which, at the same time, take account of the connections between people's positions, their personal suffering, and the structural factors impinging on their lives (Dominelli, 1988, p.156).

There is an extensive literature covering and debating the wide range of campaigning strategies that have developed within community work (e.g. Alinski, 1971; Brager and Specht, 1973; Butcher et al., 1980; Henderson and Thomas, 1980 and 1981; Smith and Pearse, 1987: Twelvetrees,1982), and it is beyond the scope of this work to review it. Instead, we use an extended group example - the Ainsley Teenage Action Group (Harrison et al., 1981; BBC, 1981) - to provide an illustration of campaigning techniques in practice and of some of the other themes we have explored thus far. It provides a 'live' example of Stage D, the 'TAKING ACTION' stage. It illustrates the development and application by users of knowledge and skills to achieve goals which they have fixed for themselves, facilitated by the workers and with the background support of a consultant. The whole process is firmly set within the values outlined in Chapter Two. Indeed, parts of it are given in the words of the young people themselves, thus according well with Principle 2 which enjoins us to give a voice to service users.

The Ainsley Teenage Action Group (ATAG)

The group started life in the autumn of 1979. A group of teenage young men had offended together on the council estate (area of dense housing rented from the local tier of government) where they lived. One or two had served sentences of custody while others were under supervision, had been fined, or simply had not been caught. Their offences had been mostly related to break-ins at local factories and the disposal of goods stolen. Their probation officer, along with a youth worker and one of the present authors, decided to help the young people to work together as a group to pursue the young people's own goal of obtaining and running youth-run leisure facilities on the estate. Rather than taking the young people out of their community and treating them on the basis of an outside professional assessment of their needs, the aim was to help the young people to understand and to deal with their own issues, on their own home ground, in their own group.

The Workers' Role: Facilitation in Practice

The workers established themselves as a trustworthy and reliable presence in the lives of the young people, working consistently to the principles in Chapter Two in that, for example, they refused to accept members' negative labels but sought their own definitions of the problems they faced, and were committed to the possibility of their taking action on these issues through the group. They continually affirmed, acknowledged and respected what the young people brought to the group, encouraging them to find their own strengths and take their own decisions; in short, treating the young people as adults not as children.

For a group to become self-determining, it is necessary for the workers to create a relaxed informal setting in which the members feel comfortable and confident. As the Ainsley Group gained momentum, ways had to be found to promote a meeting where there was a relaxed informal attitude on the one hand, and as much participation as possible on the other, without exercising undue control. Being used to being told what to do, members found it hard to discipline themselves and to control their own sessions. In the early days, some lacked the confidence to participate at all, while others dominated agressively and gathered cliques of supporters. The workers might have been tempted to use individuals as allies to try to achieve more control, but they did not consider this acceptable, ethical or, in the long run, likely to be effective.

The use of structured exercises (as outlined in the last chapter), suggested by the workers and taken on by the group, helped to some extent but was by no means the whole answer. Eventually, a system for managing these problems emerged naturally. The members came to allow themselves a wilder 'relax' session at the beginning of each meeting, followed by getting down to 'business'. This became an accepted part of the meeting routine as one of the members stated at the time: 'When we meet at the club, the first half hour we just sit round, have a drink and just general chat between ourselves. Then we get down to sorting out how we can get one step closer to getting the club and any paper work that needs doing. Any leaflets handing out we'll do them at the club.'

Sometimes the 'relax', or general discussion time, took up the whole session and no formal 'work' was done. What the workers discovered, however, was that in these informal sessions a lot of 'business' was sorted out among the young people themselves, often pulling together discussions that had taken place outside club meetings, on the street or at school. After this, the business sessions, when they took place, were productive - sharp and decisive - and exercises were used discriminatingly, to meet group purposes rather than workers' concerns about control. The workers had to recognise and accept that, on occasions, the members took decisions independently and without their awareness. They needed to tune into the wavelength of this informal but very powerful decision-making process, whereby members might reach their own separate conclusions and not feel the need to communicate to them. This really tested the workers in their determination to facilitate the group in owning its own decisions and goals.

Consultancy for the Workers

Already, this account has involved some hard decisions for the workers and the necessity to develop a new style of working and learn to make new kinds of judgements. Consultancy sessions (see Chapter Two) were essential for untangling these questions and achieving clarity about the right way forward. In the early days, much consultancy time was spent on analysing detailed worker interventions in the group (who said what to whom) but, as the group developed, more time was spent looking at the wider issues affecting the group and the workers' role. This seemed to coincide with the young people increasingly taking over the process of decision-making (as outlined above), then running their own brainstorms in the group and recognising the need to set their own plans of action.

The workers were in no doubt that it was invaluable to meet with an objective outsider who could ask pertinent questions and challenge them to find answers. It helped prevent the work drifting, assisted the handling of anxieties brought on by happenings within the group or pressures from outside (such as the rest of the workload workers carried, or agency views about the direction the group was taking), and stopped conflicts of opinion and style from becoming too personalised. Through these shared efforts, they were able constantly, in the face of constant external pressures to do otherwise, to reaffirm their commitment to young people being their own spokespeople, making their own decisions and taking action for themselves.

Boundaries between Consultancy and the Group

In view of the belief (expressed under Principle 2 in Chapter Two) that service users should control the agenda of action, it is important that the consultancy focuses on group process and not group content. The latter, in terms of group aims, and tasks to be achieved, should be up to members to decide and regulate. Workers should not slide into prejudging these issues by airing them too fully in consultancy sessions.

As outlined in Chapter Three, the boundaries between consultancy and group sessions were interestingly explored by ATAG workers and members when the notes from a planning meeting with the consultant were seen by a group member. It was agreed that the notes be brought along to ATAG meetings and made available to any member who was interested. In addition, some group members attended the planning sessions on a few occasions. Being aware, by this time, of what was discussed in the meetings, they were able to pick up on things they particularly wanted to discuss. This reflects the members beginning to cross the boundary into sharing or taking over responsibility for group process. We shall see in Chapter Six that this forms part of Stage E of the self-directed action model and can routinely be expected of, and encouraged in mature groups. ATAG members were showing themselves ready to move into this stage.

One reason why the involvement of group members in consultancy meetings did not pose particular ethical problems, and why there was not a hidden workers' agenda for members to uncover, was because the aims for self-directed groups do not include individual change. Consultancy sessions do not focus, therefore, on possible therapeutic benefits of group membership or on professional 'assessments' of individual functioning or adjustment. The only authentic reason to consider individual levels of participation in the group is in relation to members' potential contribution to selecting and achieving the goals which they themselves have set. Workers might, for example, notice that one person has been particularly withdrawn but that they have recently become more involved, showing more initiative than usual. This might be mentioned outside of the group and a decision reached to encourage this new-found confidence. In this way, performance and behaviour of group members are related to group process by those whose function is to facilitate the functioning of the group. This kind of development might equally well be mentioned in the group, particularly in a mature group, so that both workers and members can draw out the best from each other.

Division of Worker Tasks; New Approaches to Statutory Responsibilities

As was mentioned at the beginning of Chapter Two, the ability to co-work effectively, often across professional boundaries, is a fundamental skill in self-directed work. Such collaboration requires, for example, well-developed communication skills directed to the tasks in hand, full recording of group process, adequate back-up from a consultant, and the ability to channel the lessons both from what is recorded and from the professional support mechanisms back into the groupwork itself. In the Ainsley group, the worker team was concerned primarily with helping the young people to decide issues and courses of action. However, early on, it became apparent that the group needed a reference point or, as it was termed, a 'key worker' - one member of the worker team who would take primary responsibility for certain tasks outside the face-to-face work with the young people. This ensured that the young people had a contact point between meetings, and that agencies and outside bodies had a port of call if they could not link directly with the young people themselves - though the keyworker's role would then be to make this link. Also, tasks which workers undertook to do between meetings were carried out. This role was taken on by Colin, the Probation Officer.

In this role, he was also able to undertake other tasks which were part of his wider responsibilities for some group members: these were to record the fulfilment of supervision conditions, prepare court reports and, in some cases, offer family counselling. It would not have been appropriate to deal with these matters formally in the group because the agreement between workers and young people was to focus on issues and problems which concerned them collectively. On the other hand, as the group developed, individuals increasingly chose to discuss personal matters there, and the fact that court reports were being prepared provided a useful jumping-off point for important discussions about offending, the courts, the police, and the young people's experiences generally. To all intents, the resultant reports were products of group discussions.

Although it did not happen at Ainsley, in other groups the members have submitted to Court documents commenting on local conditions and the work of their group to change these, which have been appended to the official report containing an account of the offence and relevant personal details. These have been accepted, and comments from the Bench have suggested that they helped engender a view of the young person before them which put strengths before deficiencies. This provides a practical example of Principle 1 being applied through the work of the group, since negative labels have been challenged in one of the most difficult forums of all - the Courts.

These examples also illustrate the fact, discussed previously in Chapter Three, that the voluntary membership of self-directed groups does not preclude group involvement being offered to those on statutory orders, or who are subject to statutory monitoring or investigation, provided there is no actual or implied requirement that they will join the group. Some groups,however, such as the Nottingham Who Cares Group, have preferred to avoid involving workers who are currently employed in the statutory service responsible for group members. Others, including many of the self-advocacy projects, place great emphasis on remaining entirely independent of the statutory sector, occasionally to the point of not accepting funding from that source.

Asking the Question WHY: Policing on the Estate

Let us now turn to the actual collective activities of the group. The process the group went through was to ask the questions WHAT, WHY and HOW. One particular feature of their discussions gives a clear illustration of the difference it made to their ensuing actions when they asked the question WHY.

In the group's first year the number of police arrests, prosecutions, and court appearances for Ainsley young people reduced dramatically. During this period there were no official reports of group offences of burglary, theft, or taking and driving away vehicles. However, by mid 1980, the teenagers attending the group, when discussing WHAT were their concerns now, started giving vague, frustrated accounts of conflict with the local police, about being harassed and arrested on the estate for no apparent reason. Police arrest referrals to the probation service were beginning to increase and the nature of the offences were violations of public order, such as threatening behaviour, breach of the peace and abusive language; in other words, they were always offences which the police themselves can define as such. It was also noticeable that police arrest action was confined to two or three constables, one of whom was designated community constable for the estate.

The young people began to ask themselves WHY this was happening. Here, they take up their own story (BBC, 1981):

> About 5 or 6 months ago the police activity on the estate was large. I think the reason for this was when we was together on the estate we always used to keep together, perhaps about ten of us. We used to actually split into two, the younger ones and the older ones, and we used to hang about on the estate and people used to get annoyed by the presence or the noise, and the police used to come down more or less every night - clearing us off. But instead of just coming and asking us to move, we got a lot of lip, and we got pushed around a lot and, well, we resented this.

Feelings were running so high that a group of four teenagers stoned an unoccupied police car. This incident became the main focus of the next group meeting and the members decided to make representation to the sub-divisional police headquarters, to invite the senior officer responsible for police operations in the area to meet them. 'Well, what we decided to do was we contacted the local police station, because the main source of trouble was one officer.' They role-played in advance how they thought the meeting might go, and then on their own visited the police station, thus illustrating our remarks earlier in this chapter about workers not needing to negotiate on behalf of group members. 'About five of us went up, but when we got up there they was not showing much willingness to help us, so we actually had to write a letter. We invited the Chief Inspector down to tell him the problem.' They circulated interested adults asking them to give support at the meeting. 'Well, he did a lot of talking, but we did manage to get our point over, and we emphasised that this one officer was mainly to blame for the trouble, and he said he would see what he could do about it. Subsequently this police officer was moved off the estate which is really a great thing for the estate because since then the trouble has gone down, and there hasn't been so much police activity on the estate.'

The Chief Inspector not only moved the beat constable from the estate but introduced a community liaison constable to work with the group and to help with the youth club campaign. He made a bargain with the teenagers that if he made these policing changes and adopted a lower police profile in the area, he expected the group to play their part and reduce the number of incidents and neighbourhood complaints. There was clearly a good deal of mutual respect between the teenagers and the Chief Inspector. He personally attended their monthly committee meetings, put forward points raised by the teenagers, and was at times their advocate. Further conflict with the operational police was minimal. We may contrast this with the conventional responses to young people who offend - expecting them always and solely to examine *their* behaviour on the assumption that it must need changing for the better. It also provides a stark example of workers encouraging a group to set its own goals - here to change policing behaviour - rather than these being determined by workers who believe that they know best.

Digging Deeper for Underlying Causes: Asking 'WHY' Again

The changes agreed to by the police dealt with the contentious spate of recent arrests but they did not deal with the reasons why the group had come to police attention originally, before the group was ever established. The group's view on WHY this had occurred was that they had had nothing to do and nowhere to go. They now had the group to attend, but that was only a temporary measure for a few young people and did not tackle the problem itself. Longer-term action was needed.

Moving into Action

> We decided we would have a go at getting youth facilities for the teenagers of the estate. As one of the first things, the group agreed to get a petition to see if the majority of the estate agreed with us that there are not enough play facilities. We collected over 400 signatures from residents on the estate. (BBC, 1981)

The petition was preceded by a distribution of leaflets around the estate, announcing the existence of the group and its intentions. Both the leaflets and the petition forms were drawn up by members.

The next stage was to meet their elected representatives. This idea arose accidentally, when the group took the petition to the Lord Mayor's home, not realising that he lived on the same estate as themselves. Through him, they made contact with their own local Council members:

> Councillor Stone and Councillor Marshall are local Councillors for the Ainsley estate. They visited us because we

sent them a letter inviting them to come down to Robert
Shaw Primary School where we held our meetings. We
wanted them to come to look at our petition and give us
help. When they came we told them about the estate and
about the good points, but especially that there is nothing
to do for young people. We said that we had been in
trouble and are not angels. They agreed with our aims
and made plans for us to meet the Sheriff to present our
petition.

The press were told about our petition and came to one of our
meetings to find out what we were meeting for. We talked to the
pressman about the club's problems and having no place where
we can meet. The two Councillors were also present and they
told him that they supported us. They also said we had a good
chance of getting the wasteland down by the bridge for a youth
hut, which is what we would like to start with. The following
week the press cameraman came and took some pictures of us.
(Harrison et al.,1981, from group newsletter)

The newspaper article and the picture, presenting the group in
a positive light, made quite an impact locally, and members
quickly saw the value not simply of publicity, but of representing
their cause and themselves. They immediately produced a news-
sheet, the *Ainsley Youth Express* (AYE!) detailing their activities
in a series of short articles. Some of these articles (in part
reproduced above) were by members who had been written off by
teachers as illiterate. Here there are strong echoes, once more, of
Principle 1 and the need to challenge negative labels. On
completion of the draft, and after discussing the general lay-out
and subtitles, four members went to a local community printer.
While he typed the text, they laid out titles and subtitles with
Letraset and pasted up and printed off the news-sheet on an off-
set litho machine.

Their next step had the same 'outreaching' purpose and it
tackled the 'negative labels' of Principle 1 head on:

We organised a jumble sale to gain our respect back;
because people on the estate did not like us, we did not
seem to have any .... We also had a raffle of goods given
to us by firms we had written to. This and the jumble sale
raised £55 .... People who came also saw a display of our
work: a model and a map with photographs of the estate.

Using Community Arts Techniques

The jumble sale had required considerable practical and co-ordinating effort. More unusual aspects of work surrounding the jumble sale were the photographic display and the model of the estate. For the display a small group toured the estate taking black and white photos of features they regarded as significant with regard to their aim of getting a youth hut, e.g. graffiti, 'Keep Off' notices, and areas of unused land. They then developed and printed the photos at an arts and crafts centre, mounting them on display boards at a group meeting.

The model was suggested by a worker from the Education for Neighbourhood Change Unit (Gibson, 1979), based at Nottingham University, who came to visit the members. Using materials from the Unit's resource kits and with the support of the worker, they quickly built up a scale model of the estate, which in a fresh way reinforced their arguments as to what was lacking and what could be achieved.

Such 'community arts' techniques are an effective way to make abstract issues concrete and visual for the group as well as for those they need to convince with their arguments. They also give members a short term project to carry out collectively as part of a longer campaign. This means they can experience the satisfaction of successfully completing a task and getting positive feedback on their work. Items produced can include illustrated leaflets, newsletters and reports; photographic, slide or video material; posters; and models, the latter being particularly useful for campaigning on housing or planning issues and in any fight to get 'bricks and mortar' facilities. Local authorities are more willing to allow young people to become involved in the planning process than might be supposed. Many are committed to general environmental education and a minority have directly, and successfully, consulted specific groups of young people, mainly on planning decisions which had a particular effect on them (Franklin, 1989, and *Childright* , July/August, 1989, pp.8-10).

Finding Their Collective Power

A difficult period ensued when local adults, at the instigation of the local authority, tried to 'change the rules' mid-stream and take over the campaign - and during which the young people learned some hard lessons reflecting all five of the Principles set out in Chapter Two. The parents and councillors seemed unable to see beyond their negative labels (Principle 1), they would not listen (Principle 2) and they did not want to consider the wider problems underlying the sitution the young people were in (Principle 3). Above all, and despite their good efforts on improving their image, the members still keenly felt their status as an oppressed group (Principle 5) owing to prejudice against the young and against offenders: they are so readily dismissed as 'hooligans', or 'delinquents'.

Based on this recognition, and encouraged by the workers, the young people looked to themselves for collective power (Principle 4) and found their own momentum and sense of purpose again by refocusing on their original goals. They kept their overall aim in sight by running youth club sessions in the school where they held their own meetings and, since by this time some of them were aged 18 or over, were able to win back control of the club's steering committee and funding. Their building was finally opened five years after the group began. Purpose built, it was a simple but weather-proof shell with mains services, ideal for lively activity, which the members equipped themselves. Attendance regularly reached a hundred. The older group members took responsibility for the day-to-day running, supported by regular discussions with one of the workers.

Over a period of years, then, the young people had exposed the real nature of the problems they faced (WHAT) and had organised with others, combining analysis (WHY) and action (HOW), to tackle these effectively. In TAKING ACTION, they had utilised campaigning techniques which may be more familiar to community workers, planners and youthworkers than to social workers or other 'mainstream' welfare professionals. Crucially, however, they had done this in order to solve a problem - offending - which was the proper province of a statutory agency, in this case the probation service. In this general way, we aim to bridge the gap between disciplines, for instance by placing the skills and strategies of community work at the disposal of social work, wherever they hold values in common.

Anti-Oppressive Working

Although the Ainsley Group provides an excellent example of participants reaching their own analysis and taking action on this basis, it was a less successful experience for the workers in relation to anti-oppressive working. This may be partly attributed to the date the group was established since such issues were not so emphatically on the agenda at that time but this should not be taken as an excuse for workers' oversights

The seeds of the difficulties were sown in the unquestioning assembling of an all white, all male worker team. One assumes that this would be much less likely to be contemplated now than in 1979, when the group began. The workers soon found themselves confronted with sexism, homophobia *and* racism in a group which was mixed race but predominantly male (Ward, 1987). In terms of gender, the boys frequently dominated the girls through ridicule, the loudness of their voices, and pushiness. Implicitly the boys believed they had the right to behave in this way - that their interests prevailed over girls'. The boys also behaved in 'Macho' ways towards each other, using humiliation to establish and maintain a pecking order. They would react to the male workers not joining in with their views about women with mistrust and accusations that they were 'homos'. Similar views existed amongst the white members about race, although it seemed less acceptable to express these openly.

The workers struggled with ways of challenging the constant manifestations of sexism, and other oppressive attitudes. Working, as they were, at the time when the self-directed model was still emerging, their predominant focus was on keeping sight at all times of the young people's own agendas and avoiding the tendency to revert to the very type of authoritarian role they had struggled so hard to reject. Consequently, it felt awkward to point continually to behaviour and attitudes which they found unacceptable.

Yet it was not possible, either, to tolerate these and some way out of the dilemma had to be found. The least effective way would have been the single, closed response in sharp contradiction of oppressive comments. In practice, the workers operated somewhere between the two broad strategies outlined by Taylor (1984). The first was a *defensive* mode. This took place on the young people's own territory, in their group, and involved coaxing, cajoling and confronting sexism and racism, taking into account the fluctuations of the group. The workers recognised this as being loaded with compromises. Secondly, there was a more *offensive*, challenging, approach. This operated mainly in the spaces outside specific group meetings when there were opportunities for freer, more flexible forms of interaction, less overpowered by group norms, and used in contact mainly with individuals or sub-groupings.

The task for these workers was to introduce a challenging approach more consistently into all their exchanges with the young people. The example also illustrates the inherent and insurmountable weaknesses of a worker team consisting of three white males, with all the prejudices and assumptions that such a grouping unavoidably carries into practice. Dominelli (1988, p.16) highlights the difficulties for white social workers in their relationships with white users. Sympathising with their predicament can so easily amount to 'collusion engendered by their shared assumptions of white supremacy'.

The goal for all workers must be to work with appropriate others *and* to equip themselves to work in a way that confronts all social divisions, accepting the values for practice we have outlined in Chapter Two, but recognising the different starting points between people and the significance of such differences in facilitating their experiences, understandings, aspirations and opportunities. In practice, for workers, this means undergoing awareness training and learning to deconstruct the oppressive ideologies which are embedded not only in the attitudes absorbed by users but in their own personal behaviour and professional practice, and institutionalised in the procedures of their employing organisations. It also means setting up worker teams which are diverse and non-collusive in their make-up, like that of Mistry (1989), a black probation officer, and her white co-worker. Such teams will be more capable of confronting their own oppressive attitudes and behaviour, and more credible as a model of anti-oppressive relationships. They will also provide a firmer base from which to offer a consistent and unambiguous challenge to racism and sexism of the like which faced the Ainsley workers, and with which they compromised.

Summary

Overall, the Ainsley Teenage Action Group members discovered that they could become more powerful in questioning other people's attitudes towards them, and in analysing and tackling the issues which dominated their lives. They were helped to take the initiative into their own hands: by taking their own decisions in the group, finding the strengths they needed amongst their own members, learning the necessary skills and acquiring the necessary knowledge and resources to pursue their campaign.

Without question the young people learned in a very practical way how to run a fairly complex organisation, and to take responsibility for it. In so doing they learned to take responsibility for their own actions - taking decisions, sticking to them in the face of pressure from officials, councillors and other adults, and facing the consequences. On the surface this may carry echoes of the rhetoric of personal responsibility and enterprise, glibly advocated in current policies for young people. However, the context in which it has been developed, the objectives sought and secured, are a far cry from those envisaged by these policy makers.

In the process, the young people came to distinguish between helpful and oppressive adults - how to include the former and exclude the latter. In examining what they did with their time, the young people realised the problems in their neighbourhood. They became aware of the concentration of power in the established institutions, and within adults at a personal level, and how these come together effectively to disempower young people - and working class young people like themselves especially. They came to appreciate that society does not allocate resources fairly, to young people or to other powerless groups (though the work in the group on recognising the interlinked nature of oppression could have been stronger), that planning and policing policies often do not show much concern for those they most affect. However, they learned, also, that this state of affairs and those who uphold it can be challenged. Consequently, they grew in confidence and experience and earned new respect - new labels, indeed - from their families, the local community and the public authorities. The work they undertook, with the support of the groupworkers, was carried out on their own terms, focusing on their own goals, and aimed at keeping the young people themselves in control. The group itself, rather than the workers, took the credit for their own success. The participants found this self-directed process, as much as its outcome, to be an empowering one.

Chapter Six

The Group Takes Over

A Detailed Examination of Stage 'E' of the Model

Following an initial round of taking action, groups inevitably pause to take breath. Stage E begins with the group reviewing what it has achieved, coming to see links between the range of issues addressed thus far, and identifying new areas to be tackled. The group then continues with more collective action, joining or establishing new campaigns. Members turn to their own group meetings for confirmation of the wider understanding they have reached and to consolidate their feeling of shared strength and conviction. By this time, they will have redefined their experience from one of personal inadequacy and self-blame to strength and determination, through the achievement of doing something about the external factors which have contributed to their oppression. By making these connections, they realise that they have a right to a different style of services and to more control over their own lives.

The group, having always been helped up to now to analyse issues and set its agenda of action, takes over increasing responsibility for ensuring that this is done, as well as for group process. 'Changed consciousness' and 'collective power' (Hudson, 1985, p.648) are both now under members' own control. Mature self-directed groups become models to those who may be able to join together to take action in a similar way. They may feature heavily in the media and become skilled at using it as a mechanism of change as well as of publicity. The workers, meanwhile, move gradually into the background and take on a different kind of role. Alternatively, both parties may judge the time to be right for the workers to leave the group altogether. Evaluation of the group, and of the workers' performance in it, are consequently of key significance at this time.

The themes which will be covered in this chapter, then, are making the connections, using the media, evaluation, changing worker roles and withdrawal of workers.

Making the Connections

We refer to the process of evaluating past achievements, making connections between issues, and planning for the future, as reformulating the questions 'WHAT?', 'WHY?', and 'HOW?'. It is an exercise which happens numerous times in mature groups and which, indeed, becomes a continuous process. Reformulating 'WHAT?' means asking 'what are the problems we still face?' In so doing, the group members are naturally led into 'reformulating 'WHY?' - that is, asking themselves why such a range of issues exists and perceiving the links between them. As they continue to develop their understanding of the external causes which have placed difficulties in their way - in the case of the Derbyshire Coalition of Disabled People, for example, causes which relate to prevailing attitudes about, and neglect of provision for, disabled people - groups also see ways in which they can tackle further aspects of these causes in order to bring about change. This we regard as: 'reformulating 'HOW?', or 'how can we best act on our renewed understanding to achieve our demands?' As the group continues its progress - and it is now evident why self-directed groups are not short-term groups - this reformulation of 'WHAT?', 'WHY?' and 'HOW?' becomes a continuing process throughout the life of the group. Campaigns and actions continue, whilst understanding grows proportionately.

Members' developing perception, at this stage, of the injustice they face and of their own relative powerlessness, will slowly grow into a broader comprehension that they and others beyond their immediate group share the experience of social oppression. They come to see change, and action to achieve it, not as a local concession but as an absolute right. They recognise the need to make links with people in other places and to take further action, often at a regional or national level (Dourado, 1990). Group members now wish to alter the way that things are 'done to' them without their permission and to alter, too, the attitudes held by others about them.

Disabled people, for example, in a group like the Coalition, reach a stage where they are no longer prepared to tolerate, let alone to be grateful for, inadequate, stigmatizing and paternalistic forms of service delivery. At the very least, they are consumers who have a right to expect a reasonable standard of service. Going beyond that, however, with an awareness which informs them that their rights should extend as far as complete equality, they now wish to take over the actual control of the services which are essential to their full participation in a predominantly able-bodied world, and hence to take control over their own lives. 'Taking over', does not mean seizing the power to exploit those one has been exploited by in the past, but gaining the direction of one's own life and one's own affairs. Taking the first decisions for oneself breeds the desire to go on taking decisions, and to extend one's sphere of capabilities as far as it can go. It also engenders the demands to be perceived as capable and in control, not to be patronised, not to be dismissed as incompetent or uncomprehending, and not to be left out of account when the really important decisions are made or the real power is exercised.

The workers' role, now that some successful campaigning has been concluded, becomes one of helping the group to analyse what it has achieved, and why it worked; to identify the problems they still face, and the extent to which they still fall short of being fully accepted into society and given equal treatment. Workers go on to help the group plan and carry through its next project or campaign, recognising that the overall goals of at least some of the group members will have moved up several notches and will be directed at achieving a more fundamental level of change beyond short term advantages or immediate individual need. Group members will by now be generalising from what has happened to other issues which confront them. This phase of empowering practice is characterised, then, by users making connections between achievements and experiences so far, broadening out to wider concerns and, finally, moving towards 'taking over' whilst the workers move into the background.

The springboard for these developments is often the tangible success of groups *acquiring their own resources or facilities*. It is not just the fact of having a building which matters, however, but of running and managing it themselves. The *real* issue is one of beginning to have some control. The North Braunstone Womens Self-Help and Action Group, for example, fought hard to secure a women's centre for their estate. Having had an application for joint Inner Area funding rejected, they made a successful appeal to the Department of the Environment and lobbied and pressurised the local council to make its contribution. The women's group became the Steering Group and then the Management Committee of the new centre, taking fierce pride in its physical creation. Nothing was allowed into the building unless it matched up to their conception of what the centre meant to them. They tell an animated tale about the arrival of a desk for an Open Access worker, employed to develop women's access to education and training, who had been invited to be based there. A large second-hand teacher's desk, sent for her use, was considered by members to be in such a poor state that it was unacceptable to them, so they asked her to send it back. In this way, the women demonstrated their feeling of responsibility for and pride in their centre. They jointly made all the decisions about it, such as not allowing smoking upstairs where the workers' offices are (even though most of the women themselves smoke), and they were able to ask the decorator to put his cigarette out while working up there. As one member remarked, 'It's nice to have that little bit of authority'. A more notable example of the way they became able to assert their views, came when they saw the unacceptably poor quality of work on the built-in cupboards in the creche. When they saw that a local man was 'making a hash of it', the women had the confidence to write off the work already done, pay the man off, and have the job finished professionally.

In another context, the Derbyshire Coalition of Disabled People (DCDP) has achieved some enormous successes, again coming to fruition in the establishment of a Centre for Independent Living 'based on the actual experiences of disabled people who were living independently in the community' (DCDP, 1986a, p.7), where advice is available about every aspect of life as a disabled person. DCDP successfully fought against the ingrained paternalism of the local authority to gain control of substantial funds for users to run their own facility in this way. Achievements like these appear to mark the threshold between stages D and E of the model. The acquisition of their own resource provides groups with the demonstrable success which can act as a foundation and springboard for further and extended action.

The extension of the original scope of campaigning often comes when groups *link up with other people* in the same position as themselves, share their experiences and enthusiasm, and assist and advise them to develop their own organisations and campaigns. This 'multiplier' approach has been central to the development of local groups for young people in the care of the local authority, for example, and contributed to the strength of the National Association of Young People In Care (NAYPIC). The Nottingham Who Cares Group, for instance, gave numerous talks to other young people in care, and organised one of the national NAYPIC meetings.

The Ainsley group also played an active role in developing a network of youth action groups across the city of Nottingham, one of which was called upon to give evidence to the parliamentary Select Committee on Children, meeting with members of both Houses of Parliament at Westminster. Another group led a workshop on 'barriers to communication' at a conference, promoted by a leading national children's organisation, under the banner heading 'Involving children and young people'. Despite the rhetoric, this workshop was the only contribution over the three days which was organised and run by young people on their own terms, as the group members pointed out. They decided they would not try to give 'tips and hints' to adults on communication but, using empowerment techniques, 'help them to think out their own views, and how they and their agencies see young people' (Badham et al., 1989, p.3). They drew in other young people attending the conference to join with them as co-facilitators.

A natural consequence of linking with other groups, has been the expansion of activities from a local level to at least a regional or national platform. McLeod, working in one of the least auspicious of issue areas - prostitution - discusses firstly how, as a probation officer, she moved from encounters with a large number of street prostitutes on an individual basis into groupwork focusing on economic and social issues surrounding prostitution, the state of the law and the possibility of change (Longres and McLeod, 1989, p.274). From this foundation, PROS (Programme for the Reform of the Law on Soliciting) developed as a movement bringing together prostitutes from all over the country. It aimed at ending the scapegoating through the law as it stood, securing fairer treatment of women working as prostitutes, and encouraging public appreciation of the social origins of prostitution. PROS played a not inconsiderable part in bringing about changes in the Street Offences legislation and making soliciting non-imprisonable, although these changes and the continued operation of the law - for instance, by imprisoning women for fine default rather than soliciting - fall far short of meeting the women's demands.

Some campaigns have gone international and, through the collective support of secure local foundations and experience, groups have been able to have far more impact than those users who attend international forums on an individual basis and find them only bewildering and demoralising (Croft, 1989). Thus, in the course of its campaign to secure funding for the Centre for Independent Living, the Derbyshire Coalition of Disabled People became affiliated to the British Council of Disabled People which, in turn, is a member of the Disabled People's International (DPI), a grouping of organisations from nearly a hundred member states of the United Nations. DPI has campaigned to alter attitudes at the global level, including through its consultative status to the UN. This formal recognition and the benefits of coming together on an international basis (as many other groups have also found) have spurred on vigorous activity across the world.

In this context, the European Region of the DPI, like the DPI World Council, has begun to be involved in propagating the idea of Centres for Independent Living and representatives from DCDP contributed to a major conference on this topic in Stockholm (DCDP, 1986a, p.11, and 1986b), as did those from the Hampshire CIL. Indeed, there is now a national network of CIL initiatives in Britain, concerned with housing, education, employment, transport, welfare rights and other topics, and acting as advocates for disabled people in their dealings with statutory authorities. The disabled individual is kept at the centre of all arrangements and plans, and other disabled people serve on the management committee. The European Community, through its Bureau for Action in Favour of Disabled People, has also lent support to independent living initiatives, and the Derbyshire Centre is partly funded by an EC Social Fund Grant.

The Coalition, like other mature, self-directed groups, has also staged large-scale events for consumers and interested professionals. DCDP's efforts in this regard have included a whole series of disability awareness days, mainly for residential and day care staff, but also for at least one area office of social services, and with a course planned for senior County Council managers and elected members. An interesting debate is taking place as to whether changing attitudes is any use if it leaves control of services untouched. DCDP finds that being face-to-face with basic grade staff, thrashing out the practical detail of the impact of their practice on service delivery, is more rewarding than the protracted and exhausting negotiations with senior management - yet it has to be combined with the latter if it is to lead to any redistribution of power. 'It is from this growing consciousness and political power of disabled people that ultimately solutions to the problems of disability may emerge' (Oliver, 1983, p.116).

TECHNIQUES IN MATURE GROUPS - USING THE MEDIA

One of the most effective ways for groups to move from local action onto a wider canvas is through the use of the media. The Top End Youth Action Group is achieving this through having won the equal opportunities category of the Social Work Today Awards (Cohen, 1989, p.9). Similarly, the Ainsley group drew attention from the BBC through a presentation at a regional social work conference, so that they were approached to take part in a slot in the 'Grapevine' TV Series, featuring the group and its work. The student council set up by users of the AVRO Adult Training Centre in Essex (for adults with severe learning difficulties) writes letters to challenge degrading attitudes and unacceptable terminology on the part of the media, central and local government, and the general public. This has brought it features on programmes on three television channels and the council now forms part of the widespread self-advocacy movement amongst people with learning difficulties, which is challenging attitudes in as many ways as can be found. The Nottingham 'Who Cares' group was instrumental in requesting and preparing a guide for children coming into the care of the local authority, which included an explanation of their rights and what to expect from care. The group also invited the Director and Chair of Social Services to meet with it; was interviewed on the local radio; and made its own video as an introduction to its work and aims which was used whenever it made presentations to social work students, to other young people in care, and to foster parents.

Using the media requires a high level of skill, as even large statutory agencies have only relatively recently begun to learn, as does allowing oneself to be featured in the press or on television in a way that will not be damaging to the group (or the agency) itself, and which will convey the desired message as opposed to being merely newsworthy. Traditionally, much more attention has been given to working with the press (Hall, 1974; MacShane, 1979; Smith, 1981) than with radio or television. We will therefore concentrate our attention on the latter.

The danger in programme- and film-making is of meeting someone else's agenda and preoccupations at the expense of either the group's objectives or the empowerment process. A number of groups have had particularly negative experiences with television directors which in one case almost broke up the group permanently. Multi-culture, for example, a campaigning group of Punks seeking a city-centre meeting place, was approached by the director of a TV programme for teenagers to make a video about its activities. Forty-five members actively participated and put a tremendous amount of work into the production. In the event the item was cut to thirty seconds when broadcast, bitterly disappointing members, injecting self-doubt and dousing their enthusiasm for their campaign which lost momentum and took valuable time to recover. Another group, the Grandparents' Federation, gave considerable time to the preparation of a training film, only to find that its input was juxtaposed with contradictory views from another party and lost its impact.

The most basic lesson is to ask for the right to see the finished product before it is published or broadcast, and if at all possible to retain a veto on its use. Equally important is the actual process which will be used to obtain the desired material. The Ainsley group was given the opportunity over several meetings to get to know the director they worked with before filming started and to agree on the 'ground rules' for the involvement of the T.V. crew. The group was not asked to 'perform' specially for the cameras but was filmed going about its normal, everyday activities. Overall, members found their experience with the BBC Community Programmes Unit very positive and were well pleased with what was broadcast.

The timescale for the filming and also the amount of group time it will take up each week should be agreed in advance. The director should be prepared to work with the group in planning the programme or item, and should not intervene in group matters as such. If the group is able to 'vet' the director concerned and in this way finds that he or she is simply impossible to work with, it may be better to withdraw from the programme unless another director can be substituted. One group of young people in care found that they were being expected to behave in all respects as the director wanted them to, to the point where they became deskilled and lacking in confidence, and lost their sense of direction as a group. They also found that conflicts broke out between group members over how this situation was to be handled which could not be resolved because the group no longer had the privacy in which to do this. They had not negotiated with the very interventive director involved any right to ask the TV people to withdraw temporarily or to renegotiate the terms on which they were being filmed, so they were effectively stuck. A further danger is of being diverted from local issues. While the 'Grapevine' exercise did in fact help to alert the Ainsley young people to the wider significance of their campaigning - how national government policy and general public attitudes reflected on their problems - the sheer time and attention it demanded temporarily disrupted the local campaign.

A particularly common danger with the media is that they will attempt to go for the 'sob story' approach. It can be hard for members to convey to a reporter that the group finds this tone patronising and that the whole of its work represents a belief in the rights of its particular constituent group, not a wish for charity, pity or condescension. Groups such as the Derbyshire Coalition of Disabled People wage a constant battle in respect of the kind of media coverage which they and disabled people in general receive. The Coalition's Public Relations Officer co-ordinates a press cuttings service for the printed media locally and nationally, which allows her to monitor the use of her own press releases as well as other mentions of DCDP or of topics of interest to it. DCDP is attempting to ensure that television programme listings include symbols to indicate when subtitles will appear, and it has entered into correspondence with the Press Council about headlines and features which it considers to be emotive and patronising. The local television company, has been contacted about the lack of disabled people in programmes and the use of able-bodied actors to portray disabled people. Members are also urged to apply to appear on quiz shows and discussion programmes so that disabled people can be seen to be part of the general population, taking their place alongside everyone else.

The positive side of the power of the media was demonstrated when the Derbyshire Coalition reached an impasse with the County Council on the conversion of a residential unit into what became the Centre for Independent Living. The making of a TV film provided the local authority with the incentive to break the deadlock. The documentary in question, called 'Statement of Intent' (made by Central TV), took its name from the pledge which DCDP had successfully called upon the County Council to adopt in 1981, the International Year of Disabled People and refocused everyone's attention on the original principles they had wanted to adopt.

Changing Worker Roles - Handing Over to the Group . . .

As we have progressed through the stages of the model, we have seen members taking on more and more responsibility for the group. They increasingly share with paid workers (and, in DCDP's case, key office holders) in what Longres and McLeod (1980, p.271) refer to as 'the process of discovery, development and change', whilst the worker encourages them to believe in the capabilities they so obviously possess. The worker task changes from an emphasis on structuring the decision-making process, to creating space and opportunities for group members to work autonomously.

An example of this change of direction took place with the Kennington Road Action Group of young people in Nottingham. On the first occasion when the group members ran a summer holiday activity scheme, the workers had to assist members in detail on all aspects of the planning and running of the scheme using the 'taking action' techniques outlined in previous chapters. The next time round, the workers stayed in the background and played a more advisory role. In direct terms, they only needed to provide, or to point members towards, information on local authority grants and other sources of funding, and on the practicalities of running their scheme. This left members free to consolidate and extend the skills and awareness they had developed previously.

To be sensitive to these changes and to adapt their practice accordingly, workers need to be on their toes - using evaluation processes to stay alert to the way the group is evolving. The very same questions which lie at the heart of empowerment work with users form the framework of evaluation:

> What are the issues and problems users face?
> Why do these problems exist?
> How can we as workers enable users to achieve change?

> (Social Action Training, 1989, p.9)

By the time that Stage E of a self-directed group has been reached, the groupworkers are occupying a far less central role (Heap, 1988). Group members themselves have become increasingly skilled in relation both to group task performance and group maintenance or 'process'. Consequently they take much more of the responsibility for moving the group forward than hitherto. There may still be times when the workers move to the fore again temporarily (Brown, 1989). For example, a group may hit the doldrums for a period, or it may become static simply because members are enjoying the performance of tasks for their own sake rather than as a means to an end, or because the social pay-offs of group membership have caused them to lose sight of their longer term aims. Generally, however, in a group which has 'made it' through to this stage, such episodes are short lived. A brief return to the use of earlier planning and action techniques will get the group back on course.

As groups mature, they become able to spot and handle problems like these over group 'process' by themselves. A good example of this is provided by the experiences of the North Braunstone Women's Self Help and Action Group. In fighting for the resources to set up its 'Turning Point' Women's Centre, the members had found their strength and identity as a group to be a crucial asset. Then, when the group became transformed into the Steering Group to establish the Centre, some members were frightened off by the complexities of a City Council course on acting as employers and left the group. Members realised from this how much support and development a *new* member would need before she could join them as a full partner in their current responsibilities, and they knew that they did not have the time or the capacity to offer that level of support during this period. Consequently, they took the decision themselves to close the group until the Centre opened. If anyone had joined at this juncture without massive support - which they could not offer during this period - she would have become totally perplexed by all the talk of constitutions, job descriptions, and other aspects of employing and managing staff. This would have been a confidence-sapping, not a confidence-building experience. As one of the members put it: 'new people wouldn't get confident in this group'.

... and Withdrawing

Although we have constantly stressed the open-ended nature of involvement in self-directed groups, eventually the workers may need to judge when it is appropriate to withdraw completely from the group. Even if they were the initiators, the workers do not necessarily need to continue for ever. However:

> Letting go of almost anything you have been instrumental in starting is not easy. When a carers' group moves from being social worker led to member run, everyone - both

members and professionals involved - needs to think through the issues.

Professionals . . . often have unreal expectations about this sort of change. They underestimate the complexity of it and the time it will take. (Wilson, 1988, p.34).

When a group is contemplating becoming self-sustaining, action and direction, like participation, require formal and explicit structures based on democratic principles (Freeman, 1970, pp.7-8). These include delegating responsibility and distributing authority to those best able to handle it, rather than to the most popular or most dominant individuals - as was done in the North Braunstone group by electing a quiet but efficient woman to the Chair - and rotating tasks, as various groups have done with the minute-taking. The group itself, according to Freeman, needs to determine who will exercise power and authority and who will have access to information, and to share both as widely as possible.

This is a two-way process. As the members gain more autonomy, the worker too must be preparing to release control and moving out of the 'central person' role (Heap, 1966). This needs to be done in a skilled and measured way, giving attention to both practical and feeling aspects of the group's functioning. Rather than a uniformly paced withdrawal, letting go involves the skill of gauging when the group has become sufficiently self-motivating and self-resourcing for the workers' contribution to its functioning, at both task and emotional levels, no longer to be essential (Heap, 1988, p.27). Unless the group has become resourced from within the local community, or has achieved its purpose and is drawing to an end, it is crucial for the workers to make a realistic assessment of the group's strengths and functioning at the time, not arising from a pre-determined idea of what is appropriate in general terms. The Rowland Dale Group, (which did not long outlive its workers leaving, following a scheduled number of weeks of worker facilitation) provides an example of two common misconceptions - that worker withdrawal should be built into the planning of a group in advance, and that it is a 'once and for all' activity.

At the other extreme, the Rock and Reggae Festival, referred to in Chapter Two, gradually became a self-sustaining event over a period of ten years, with the youth worker moving into a background, consultative role. Although many of the bands that played in the early festivals remained involved in its organisation, a new generation came forward to take responsibility and new performers were found every year.

> Every year there is a question over whether it will happen but it always comes together in the end. The healthy aspect of this instability is that it forces those remaining to undertake new recruitment. This requires fresh publicity and open meetings. It puts responsibility for the event back within the local community, avoiding it becoming the slick operation of a small clique. (Social Action Training, 1989, p.43)

Similarly, in the Ainsley group, once the youth facility was under way, and running successfully, it was decided with the young people that two of the three original workers should withdraw. The probation officer remained involved in an enabling role, dictating neither pace nor decisions to the group members. He saw himself, rather, as being there to support them in their decisions, and to help them move forward if they got stuck.

Prejudgements about withdrawal (Wilson, 1988) make no more sense in groupwork than they would in casework. Self-directed groups tend to be long-term and to require an extended process of withdrawal as well as of development. If the workers leave prematurely or too precipitately, the group will be badly shaken and may even fold.

Evaluation

To avoid such misjudgements, the skill of evaluating past performance must be central to the last stage of the self-directed approach. However, it is too late at this juncture for workers and members to learn the skills involved, or to establish the necessary responsiveness to constructive criticism and suggestions. To be effective, evaluation needs to be emphasised from the start and not seen as predominantly a feature of terminating work (Brown 1986; Preston-Shoot, 1988).

Evaluation of the Group

Maintaining the emphasis on full participation by users, the evaluation of the group as it enters Stage E will be conducted jointly by workers and members. In any approach which aims to be member-centred, joint evaluation must be a key constituent. The workers in self-directed groups have to be prepared to raise the purposes and objectives of their activities, and inevitably the values which these are intended to represent, to open and specific scrutiny. Both workers and members need to develop evaluative skills, so that they are able to comment on their own and each others' work to date and to become more effective as a result.

The broad questions to be asked in evaluating the group's work to date cover all the steps in Stages B, C and D of the model: whether the group was planned in an open and shared way; whether, with appropriate facilitation by the worker team at all points, the group succeeded in setting its own agenda of issues and analysing why the problems on this agenda exist; whether they decided clearly what action to take, and effectively broke it down into a series of tasks which were then shared out between themselves and carried through efficiently. At the same time, there needs to be consideration of whether members' expectations have been met in the group, whether it has achieved its aims, whether members have found the method used to be an effective and appropriate one, and whether changes or further developments are required.

It is important to bear in mind that both group task and group process should feature in the evaluation. Co-operative working of the sort involved in self-directed groups takes place at the meeting-point between the need for task achievement - that is, for doing something concrete and visible - and the needs of individuals and of the group. The inter-relationship between establishing a secure emotional climate on the one hand, and effectively carrying out practical tasks on the other, will no doubt emerge from this process of review and evaluation.

Reflecting this inter-relationship, as influenced by the particular values of empowerment, certain issues will come to the fore in considering how far the group's aims have been achieved: have members gained more choice and greater control over matters which clearly contributed to the forces which are oppressive to them, constraining their potential and life chances; are they being treated with greater dignity and responsiveness by existing facilities and institutions, indicating a change of approach in significant people towards the user group? Such changes are unlikely to encompass everybody in an agency or geographical area who had previously devalued or discriminated against the user group, but they can begin a process of positive 'labelling' among those who have the capacity to block or open opportunities for users. In saying this, we are very clear that such labels or images are not characteristics of the members, nor is it their responsibility to change. Rather, that responsibility lies with the oppressor - for instance racism is a white problem, sexism a male problem - but one measure of success of empowerment work is to see the labellers, the image makers, beginning to change. And it is behaviour rather than attitudes that counts, as reflected in provisions, resources and procedures. If taken as the primary focus, attitudes can provide an excuse for liberal posturing which merely marks continued oppression and discrimination in practice.

To be consistent with the values of empowerment, a measure of any gains made by users on their own behalf, often in the form of new or changed facilities, should be the availability of these to people outside the campaigning group. How far are they under democratic control and seen by the wider community as 'theirs'? It is no use acquiring provisions by the sweat and toil of users, which become merely a reflection of the oppressing institutions they have been challenging, nor simply to replace one group of oppressors with another, perhaps more insidiously because it can be masked as local control but merely be doing the authorities' job for them on unchanged terms. If the Ainsley youth hut had not been widely used and democratically run by local young people, it would have offered little improvement over existing facilities.

What we have not included here is explicit evaluation of group mood or 'problems' (Douglas, 1976, p.99), defined in terms such as 'flight', 'apathy' and 'inadequate decision-making'. There are two interconnected reasons for this. Firstly, in empowerment work, such features are of no relevance in their own right; the work is externally, not internally focused. Secondly, such factors cannot be measured independently but as part of the progress of work on the group's main objectives. Hence, they are subsumed within such questions as those raised above about achievement of goals such as the acquisition of more resources and users experiencing less oppression, discrimination and devaluing behaviour.

There are examples, which illustrate this in the life of the Ainsley Teenage Action Group. Members became demoralised, with a dropping off of attendance and enthusiasm, when it appeared that control of their campaign to get a youth hut was being taken over by a committee dominated by adults, set up in that form on the insistence of the County Council Youth Service as potential funders. Similarly, they were disorientated, with decision-making effectively neutered, when a local Councillor, whom they had come to view as an ally, described the group members as 'offenders' in a newspaper interview. Among members, there were conflicting feelings of furious anger and deep hurt. It was task-focused activities, using techniques outlined earlier, which enabled them to overcome such knock-backs by analysing the issues that underlay the events and planning to take action to deal with them.

EVALUATIVE TECHNIQUES

Techniques for carrying out group evaluation, then, include all those which were listed in Chapter Four as suitable for focusing on goal selection and task performance; these are equally appropriate for this re-assessment of the group's progress and of the remaining issues it should tackle. Douglas (1976, pp.106-116) and Preston-Shoot (1988) provide details of additional techniques which may be adapted. The use of techniques will be different in Stage E groups, in that the workers have by now receded more into the background. The group members are more likely to conduct their own brainstorms, write out their own statement cards, draw their own grids, and so on, with encouragement from the workers if needed. Brown (1986, p.106) stresses the need to include some written as well as verbal feedback 'because group pressures may inhibit individual statements', and the techniques listed cover both.

One technique which we have found particularly effective in our own practice is the concentric circle exercise, outlined for another purpose in Chapter Four. In the context of evaluation, the circles can be used to represent a greater or lesser achievement of aims, with the 'bull's eye' obviously representing one hundred per cent success. Members, either individually or as a group, can plot on the circles the point any particular task has reached. Different judgements of this can be compared over time or, even more graphically, the sheet of paper can be marked periodically with arrowed lines going inwards or outwards, showing the progress of action towards its goal.

A variation on this is the thermometer representation, used frequently by fund-raisers, where the bottom can represent the starting-point of a group's work and the top the goal. The disadvantage with this is that, on a single sheet, it is difficult to show the ups and downs in any campaign that involves more than the cumulative acquisition of resources.

Evaluation of the Members

Unlike traditional practice, self-directed groupwork does not involve an individualised evaluation of each member's progress in the group. The goals of the intervention concern the group as a whole and their achievement or otherwise needs to be measured at that level. Although there is no doubt that individuals develop both practical and social skills, it is axiomatic to the approach that these are seen as secondary and not primary outcomes. It is our view that this *must* be so. So strong are wider social pressures towards 'blaming the victim', that to allow personal developments to have undue significance would be a dangerous step back towards patronising and pathologising orientations.

Evaluation of the Workers

In traditional groupwork, the workers normally evaluate their own performance. At the most, they may seek limited comments from members to feed into this process, typically through a closing evaluation exercise at each meeting. An example of this would be a round of 'Resent and Appreciate' whereby each member in turn is asked to say one thing they resented or disliked about that week's session and one thing they liked or appreciated. The workers might keep notes on the responses and feed these into their own subsequent evaluation of the group. In self-directed groups, on the other hand, the underlying belief in partnership makes it far more important to carve out a central role for the members throughout the process of evaluation, including the evaluation of the workers.

In Chapter Five, we gave an example from the Ainsley Teenage Action Group which demonstrated how workers undertaking an evaluation of their own performance with their consultant were challenged to include the group members. In the process, they re-examined their views on the matter and discovered that there was a fundamental contradiction between their talk of openness in the group and their separation of their own learning from that which they expected of group members.

The sorts of issues which are considered in the groupworkers' performance, just as much as the way this is done, should reflect the central tenets of the self-directed approach. Hence, values will need to occupy a key place in *what* is being evaluated as well as in *how* it is measured. There might, for example, be a detailed examination of the 'fit' between the worker team's expressed value position and the way in which they have actually related to group members. It is by no means uncommon for workers to talk about working in partnership while in fact constantly reinforcing their own, more powerful position. Conversely, workers may find that they have been able, over time, to move closer to what empowerment requires from their practice, or to reach a more mature statement and realisation of their values.

It can, of course, be most instructive to chart this development. Detailed points to consider might include the extent to which each worker, and all the workers together, have been able to become more open with group members; better able to help them set their own goals; increasingly alert to what is a 'normal' response to adversity through group members' eyes; more aware of the need for, and more effective in fighting for improved resources, both through, and outside of the group; and generally more skilled in this type of groupwork. Beyond this, each worker may fruitfully consider the extent to which their wider practice, including with individuals, has changed as a result of their involvement in the group. Have they moved towards a more open and shared style of working, for example, and have they shown greater willingness and ability to refer people on, when they feel ready, to other user-led groups or projects in the community?

Concluding Comments

The effect of self-directed groups which run their course through to maturity is both deep and far-reaching. On meeting people who have belonged to such groups, it is clear what an impact their involvement has made. It has provided a framework for understanding, and experience and skills for handling, the personal and wider relationships of the society in which they are living, even in the face of unemployment, poverty, racism, and the other evils of contemporary society.

The groups also provide an opportunity to experience 'an alternative culture' (Rowbotham et al.,1979) in which people are able to pool ideas and grow together towards an understanding of how they and others like them are oppressed, but also of how they can fight back, and support one another during the emergence of a new way of thinking and responding. In our society's dominant culture, users are expected to vie against and outdo one another in being more deserving. The self-directed approach has helped to show that people can have completely different priorities and values, cooperating with, and relying upon one another, whilst working towards real improvements and change.

Finally, in 'taking over', groups make an impact far beyond members' immediate lives and surroundings. They provide ideas and support to others to aim for similar achievements. Their success and visibility makes space for new groups to go in the same direction, and thus contributes significantly to developments which will see empowerment spread more widely.

Chapter Seven

Taking It Forward

We have aimed in this book to reach practitioners who feel they want to make changes to the way they relate to service users. We have argued the relevance of the self-directed model across professional settings and have considered the necessary trans-formation of traditional working practices to reflect a set of essential practice principles. These have been translated into a five-stage model which has been explored in some depth.

In this closing chapter, we shall reflect on possible obstacles to the adoption of self-directed work, such as the apparent inapplicability of the approach in some circumstances or a lack of agency support. We will also consider ways in which these may be countered. In conclusion, the role of self-directed groupwork at the heart of empowerment will be re-emphasised, and its potential impact hinted at in training and research, as much as in practice.

Application of the Model

We believe that the self-directed model has an immensely wide applicability; indeed, that there is no reason, in terms of its effectiveness and its ability to encompass the complex causation of contemporary social problems, why it should not become the norm for helping intervention, leaving currently more accepted approaches on the periphery. We shall therefore consider the possible limitations to its use rather than arguing, instance by instance, where it could be introduced. We would then argue that in all other circumstances it should at least be considered.

What, then, are the possible restrictions on the use of the self-directed approach in practice and are these apparent or real? In some instances, arguments have been put to us that it would be of only narrow usefulness and these we reply to here.

Organisational Contexts

Of course it sounds easy to write, as we have done in earlier chapters, about offering service users a more empowering style of intervention. It is far harder, we realise, to make the necessary changes in one's practice and all that surrounds it, even when the need for change is obvious to practitioners and users alike. There are, for example, frequently restrictions which lie within the worker's employing organisation:

> Some agencies are hospitable to empowerment as a goal. Others are not. Some don't know because they have never faced a situation which challenged their values to any serious degree. Agency culture grows over time, often starting with a very positive philosophy about human dignity and meeting needs. Then, under the accretions of paper work, over-worked staff, ill-tempers, rigid conformity to rules - to say nothing of difficult clientele and intractable problems, policies begin to change - both formal and informal ones - and the clients begin to receive a disservice . . . . For many reasons, clients can find themselves feeling utterly frustrated and helpless in dealing with an agency whose mission is ostensibly to serve them. (Pernell, 1986, p.112)

It may be assumed that it is prohibitively difficult to persuade *any* organisation to allow its employees to introduce empowering groups and projects into their workload, particularly where the norm is individual work. There may not be open refusal, but agencies are skilled at absorbing and diluting new ideas in accord with their own norms (Cohen, 1975, p.92), demanding compromises and spinning out decisions until all momentum is lost. As Stock Whitaker points out (1975, p.426), 'covert resistance' - verbal assurances without active support - can be far harder to deal with than out-and-out opposition because it may emerge only gradually and be quite subtle in its manifestations. She gives the example of an agency where key powerful personnel absent themselves from staff meetings thus rendering an external facilitator impotent to effect change. The Nottingham Patients Councils Support Group found that a similar thing happened in early Hospital Council meetings. These opportunities for patients' representives to meet with senior managers were sabotaged by more junior colleagues being sent along or by a complete failure to attend, sometimes without apology. This issue had to be taken up urgently with management before users lost faith in the whole notion of collective self-advocacy.

A different kind of organisational hindrance to the development of any group-based approach is the tendency in field social work and probation settings to see groups as a kind of 'optional extra'; as something to be 'tacked on' to an already heavy and demanding caseload. Groupwork is only regarded as a basic part of the job for specialist practitioners in limited areas of work such as fostering and alcohol abuse. This is all the more regrettable, given the fact that the self-directed groupwork approach has so much to recommend it both to workers and to users. Equivalent restrictions of perspective exist elsewhere, for example in mental health settings, where groups are often the result of individual specialism or interest rather than routine practice. In some professional contexts, such as hospital-based nursing, teaching, and residential work, there are 'groups' of patients, pupils, or residents already to hand. Even here, however , the tendency is to direct work purely at individual needs. It demands a special effort to step back and consider the potential of the group *as* a group. Brown and Clough (1989), for example, represent a rare attempt to apply groupwork concepts to group living settings. Once that leap of conceptualisation has been made, the possibilities for empowering intervention become virtually endless.

Certainly, some workers *have* experienced problems in persuading their agencies or managers to permit this shift to a group-based approach based on a broader social analysis, particularly in relation to very 'sensitive' user groups, such as the parents in the Rowland Dale group who had been accused of abusing their children. Often, however, those categories of service users who are seen as 'difficult' to work with or resistant to change - as are many of the oppressed groups with whom self-directed groupwork is most successful - are precisely those for whom management is likely to be readiest to accept an alternative approach which may have something new to offer. Any fresh ideas that can enthuse workers to try again may be welcome in the agency, and particularly ones which can be 'sold' as having been successful elsewhere. Whether for this reason or others, Probation management was supportive of the Ainsley Group, and other groups which followed it both in the community (Badham et al., 1988) and in penal settings (Badham, 1989). It is certainly well worth putting together a good case to persuade management of what the approach has to offer and how it can be used in a particular instance. To second guess the response with the untested plea: 'management would *never* let us try that here' is certainly never justified, since there is frequently more space in which to operate than is assumed and, even where there is not, it is morally more acceptable to look, and if necessary campaign, for more freedom of activity than to collude with its absence. As Pernell (1986, p.112), drawing on Solomon's work on black empowerment, has said of any agency's service delivery system:

> The importance and potential that it might be changed from obstacle course to opportunity system requires of workers who identify the need for change a search for their own powers of persuasiveness, of diplomatic skill, of assessment of accessibility and leverage points for inducing modification of current practices.

When people ask whether change is possible within organisations, the question can be turned back onto them: are they content to be part of the problem, as perceived by service users, or are they prepared to be part of the solution? This may involve taking on the agency, in the form of one's own middle managers or colleagues, beyond the normal negotiations and written proposals and resource requests, either at the start or when the group begins to move into sensitive issues, but this would not be done purely on one's own initiative. It would be determined as a necessary course of action by workers and service users together, usually after extensive discussion with the workers' consultant. Other agencies beyond one's own employer can also present obstacles. Funding bodies are a frequent bugbear, as was seen in the Ainsley Group account. In the case of one black youth group which wanted to produce a 'What's On' magazine (Ward and Harrison, 1989), the heavy demands from the local council to produce information, without support or resources during the process, caused the group to fold, ironically just when funding was finally granted.

Of course, workers who do refuse to turn back when they confront organisational roadblocks run straight up against issues of power. In this respect, the keystone of self-directed groupwork - that responsibility for determining the purposes and goals of the group should lie with the group members - is both a help in eventually finding a path through the quandaries of power dilemmas, and a reason why staff at all levels may initially lack the courage to attempt to employ the model. It can look like very unsafe ground. As a worker, however, one has to decide whether to be a channel for the achievement of essential change on behalf of, and in conjunction with service users, or whether to ally oneself with the obstacles to that change. If the agency demands that its workers 'be realistic' about what it is possible to change, whose reality is to be preferred - their's or that of their service users?

It is often helpful to return to the principles for practice set out in Chapter Two and to remind oneself why these seemed so important when discussed in the safety of abstract discussion and why we have to advocate for users when they are written off or ignored. Faced with the reality of office politics these values become more, rather than less vital:

> Sometimes, clients working as a group make demands on the agency.. [which] may be perceived as awkward or excessive. In such instances, the social worker who represents both the agency's goals and the group's goals can be in a difficult position. However, these kinds of interaction can help the agency to become more responsive to the needs and attitudes of its consumers. (McCaughan, 1977, p.162)

It is not possible to show respect for service users without being prepared to challenge the forces which oppress them - even if this includes one's agency. Feeling the collective strength of the group and hearing the views of service users, reaffirming one's original intent and pressing forward for further change, should be enough to boost one's flagging resolve.

ANTI-OPPRESSIVE PRACTICE
One essential area of organisational change, which points strongly towards a major role for self-directed groupwork, is the essential commitment of workers and worker teams to developing effective anti-oppressive practice. There is an urgent need to develop, for example, far more women-only projects and projects run by black service users facilitated by black workers. These, in turn, can feed back into management of services to make these more culturally appropriate.

An example is provided by a group for Asian college students. In response to an urgent call from the local public library to 'do something' about a group of Asian young people who were 'hanging around' and causing a nuisance there. Project Pehchan, a team serving Asian young people and their families, sent one permanent worker and one social work student to meet with the young people concerned. It transpired that they were students at the nearby further education college, who felt that they actually needed an opportunity to hold meetings of Asian young people at the College, but that neither the staff nor the other students would support this request. Project Pehchan's policy (Lunn, 1989, p.14) is, firstly, to help people find 'creative and positive' solutions to their own issues rather than accepting being seen as the problem and, secondly, 'to help other agencies take on board the aspirations and expectations of the Asian community', rather than itself becoming 'a dumping ground for "Asian problems" '. With the help of the two workers, then, the group defined its own goals and fed these back to the College authorities: they successfully negotiated for a place to meet on the premises, during normal timetabled hours, and also raised the questions of racist attacks by white students, and of the racism embedded in staff attitudes and in the organisation of the College.

Opening up such opportunities through all-black groups is only one aspect of anti-oppressive practice in agencies, however. Often, when new black, feminist, lesbian or gay workers have been brought in as a result of equal opportunities policies, they are then subjected to the racism, sexism and homophobia that pervade employing agencies. This can include not being given a clear brief, being expected to achieve miracles overnight, and not being provided with adequate support mechanisms. Black workers may be expected to act as 'cultural experts', which, in practice, marginalises race issues and switches attention away from white and institutional racism. Such problems have to be confronted and dealt with jointly by *all* workers who want their practice to be empowering, using their collective strength. We must all recognise the necessity to address oppressive practice by our agencies, our colleagues and management. We all have to own the responsibility for positive action and change. Every organisation, worker team and group needs a statement embodying its commitment to anti-oppressive practice and this must, like all our underlying principles, be integral to everything we do.

SUPPORT SYSTEMS
Where workers have to put up a fight to get the self-directed approach itself and anti-oppressive ideals accepted, they also need to use their shared strength to form an alliance for progress: 'Workers, too, sometimes need empowerment, which may require a group of their own, joining common cause to use their collective concern and skills to attempt to bring about change' (Pernell, 1986, p.112). They may have to struggle to be taken seriously and not to let new developments be stifled - the two social

workers who started the group for women on the North Braunstone estate which grew into the Turning Point Women's Centre, for example, were assumed to be 'raging feminists' and were dismissed out of hand by many people - or they may simply feel that they would benefit from mutual support and the opportunity to bounce ideas off one another.

Persuading the whole team to try the approach or to lend its support is one way of finding collective strength. It also ensures that groups do not fade away when particular enthusiasts leave the office, thus damaging the credibility of this way of working, and that the values underpinning the work can be carried across into other areas of work, including individual contact. Establishing a self-directed action special interest group for interested individuals across teams, agencies and/or disciplines provides an alternative where the rest of the team is not in accord. Where the agency cannot offer inspiring supervision, setting up a peer support group, a peer supervision scheme, or a formal or informal consultancy arrangement, can all be invaluable, as can attending relevant conferences, courses and practice exchanges. Women's groups have proved to be a particularly useful form of support system amongst workers whose feminist perspective is at variance with the dominant stance of their agency (Dominelli and McLeod, 1989, p.120). Issues to be resolved with management, as highlighted by Dominelli and McLeod (ibid., pp.121-122) include the right to meet in work time, to 'own' the group's agenda, and to comment on agency policies. For the lucky ones whose agencies do approve the developments they propose (as the Save the Children Fund is currently doing for social action groups amongst young people, for example), a development panel involving management staff from key involved agencies (McCaughan, 1985, p.16) could be another useful structure to adopt.

Support groups can themselves use the self-directed approach to ensure that decisions are the shared responsibility of the whole group and that staff feel empowered and justified in pursuing their own issues. Furthermore, all the techniques described in Chapter Four, such as the force-field analysis, can be used to assess and bring about the necessary process of winning more support within the agency. The chief problem encountered by those who have introduced self-directed action into their work has not tended to be marginalisation by the employer - there is no evidence of workers getting into very hot water as a result of using the model - but the isolation of moving into new areas. Networking is the obvious answer to this. It assists in developing the skills, not only to carry out self-directed work, but also to handle organisational constraints. In this way, the working environment can be manipulated to ease the group's way without losing the integrity of the work.

Consultants who are experienced in the use of the model can often open up fresh networks through their own contacts; they can provide a mechanism for reviewing the variety of contacts with like-minded practitioners and trainers outside of the group which can be crucial in the development of support. A pool of people with experience of self-directed action can thus be drawn together who are able to offer consultancy services to one another, to form worker teams to help new groups to develop, and to set up cross-fertilisation of knowledge and skills (Social Action Training, 1989). In this way, the approach continues to grow and develop, to be more widely known about and used, and to be more effective in its results. Consultants may be the crucial links in the chain who turn the bright ideas of isolated practitioners into the co-ordinated development of a new practice-theory.

USERS AS ALLIES

The other allies who should never be forgotten if a campaign becomes inevitable to protect the approach once in use, are the group members themselves. Our experience of occasions when group members have obtained the opportunity to speak to managers or others about how helpful they have found self-directed groupwork to be, and how they want to see it retained in the agency, has been startling. Group members typically do not mince words and they are the supreme experts on why the group is needed and what it has achieved for them. In addition, their blunt and forthright style tends to throw management off balance. Yet, at the same time, managers have not developed an armoury against service users as negotiators, so that they often fall into the trap of being patronisingly nice and may readily concur with demands for which workers would be rebuffed. Users also have the immensely powerful weapon always at their disposal of threatening to attract adverse publicity against the agency, which workers cannot do. Indeed, group members have a generally much wider sphere of operation open to them in this sort of situation and we should not be afraid to let them fight the good fight on their own behalf.

The most effective thing the group facilitator may be able to do is to help members to rehearse their proposed negotiation but without putting words into anyone's mouth or, we must emphasise, leading the group in any direction which it has not itself suggested. To avoid the latter danger, we have not suggested harnessing the support of potential group members to argue why the agency should allow a group to be established in the first place. Although there may be times when this is appropriate, it is hard to see how people can advocate for something they have never tried and many potential members will need the experience of the group itself before they are confident or articulate enough to campaign on its behalf. To some extent, also, the potential group members cannot be approached with a truly free choice about opting into the group or not, unless and until the worker has cleared away a good deal of the undergrowth of potential agency opposition. A worker cannot, in fairness, invite someone to come along to a group, telling them they will be free to join in setting any agenda of issues and action they choose, only for them to find that the first time the group opens its mouth it is blocked by management.

There may appear to be a certain circularity of argument here, in that the worker is being asked to predict what members' concerns are likely to be, so as to negotiate enough space for the group to have the necessary autonomy, and yet to leave members entirely free to set their own agenda. The answer probably lies in not making rigid predictions, while taking on enough of the responsibility for initial negotiation to give the group a reasonably clear run at the start. For example, there would be as little point in lulling the agency into believing that a self-directed group of young offenders was at no time going to question the behaviour of the police, as in lining up an interview for them with the Chief Constable before the group had even started.

STATUTORY AND VOLUNTARY SETTINGS
The view has sometimes been expressed to us that the self-directed model is only applicable in the voluntary sector where practitioners are assumed to have more time and freedom to indulge new ideas, away from the limiting factor of statutory involvement. Of course, this ignores funding and staffing pressures in voluntary organisations but that is another story.

It is true that, in response to workload pressures and resource constraints, statutory agencies frequently adopt ways of rationing services which are in conflict with the open membership and open-ended nature of self-directed groupwork (Badham et al., 1985; Ward, 1987). Self-directed groups throw open the doors in a way which is difficult to predict and which, on principle, should not be controlled. Many of the people who become involved in such groups have had no prior contact with the agency; not only do they make new demands, but they cut across gate-keeping procedures which may be aimed at keeping people 'out of the system'. One way round this may be to ensure that users only have a formal link with the worker's employing organisation in instances where this is a statutory requirement. Other members join the *group* rather than entering into a relationship with the agency. Since workers frequently represent more than one agency, matters of organisational accountability will need to be negotiated in any case - the collective nature of groupwork has always posed problems in this regard - and this topic can simply be added to the agenda. Alternatively, Manor (1989, pp.117-120) advocates what he calls 'multiple accountability' across agencies. Although his model is built around a very traditional, 'top down' conception of groupwork, there are elements which are close to self- directed practice - such as being at the apex of a network - and which may merely need discussing with agency managers to answer their concerns. Working from the axiomatic principle that members of self-directed groups should be fully involved in any discussions about them, an incorporative approach must be a better means of managing accountability than conventional managerial supervision which would exclude them. Feedback to the employer on the effectiveness of the work, particularly in preventative terms, is also perfectly possible - as was demonstrated in Chapter Six, in the section on evaluation. The work need not, therefore, be 'invisible' as far as the agency is concerned.

There have, in fact, been many successful examples of the self-directed approach in the statutory sector. This has happened, in many cases, despite the fact that the workers were starting from scratch and hence needed to find sufficient space and autonomy to establish the groups. Furthermore, some groups, such as the Rowland Dale Group for parents accused of abusing their children, have consisted entirely of members with whom the worker has had a statutory involvement. There have even been exciting examples in penal settings. A racially mixed group of inmates in one young offender institution, for example (Badham, 1989), was able to reach a high level of social analysis -

considering the relationship between social class and severity of sentence, for instance, and whether the workings of the law put property before people - and to take some practical steps towards change, such as inviting the principal governor to a meeting to answer questions. The group discussed a range of issues, such as the apparently unfair workings of temporary release and parole systems, the latter being taken up in a session attended by visitors from the Parole Board. Both racism and sexism were challenged in the group from the beginning, and a worker team which was balanced along race and gender lines and which crossed the agency boundaries of probation and youth work was eventually achieved. The groupwork continued for eighteen months. Although its demise in part reflected a lack of appreciation by management of its achievements and potential, it had, by then, amply illustrated that considerably more 'space' exists in agencies for innovative development than is commonly assumed.

The workloads of statutory agencies are full of groups of people experiencing oppression for whom self-directed work would open up new horizons. Groups aiming to help users look behind the reasons for their habitual calls upon a demoralising office duty system, for example, have been run both in probation (Fullerton, 1982) and in social services (Moseley, 1987/88). In the heart of mainstream social services' child care work, there are many groups in existence which tackle the issues confronting children and young people in the care system, as well as their parents and grandparents. Page and Clark (1977) give the background to groups for those growing up in care. The work of the National Association of Young People In Care, for example, over a twenty year period, has been designed to improve conditions in care and after care, to make information and advice available to those in care, to promote their views and opinions, to help to start, support and develop local groups, and to educate the public on all aspects of the needs and views of young people in care. The Black and In Care Group runs from a Manchester base and produces a monthly newsletter called *Black is Beautiful*. These groups are run *by* young people *for* young people and they have influenced the development of child care policy both locally and nationally.

Parents' groups are of many kinds, notably the Parents' Aid groups for parents of children in care which are supported by the Family Rights Group, and which have achieved a number of changes in UK child care law through campaigning in the European Court and elsewhere. Other work undertaken has included the preparation of guides covering the care system and the provision of an advocacy service to accompany parents attending reviews and case conferences. A similar range of activities is undertaken on behalf of grandparents of children in care or lost to them through adoption by the Grandparents' Federation (Tingle, 1989). There have also been groups for parents accused of abusing their children, such as the Rowland Dale Group which took a social structural view of the causes of abuse, and a number of telephone counselling and other organisations run by parents for parents who may be subject to these and other pressures.

In the rest of social services' work, the scope for self-directed groups is boundless. To take an issue which swallows major amounts of time, for example, the needs of sexual abuse survivors can be well met using this approach (Jonsdottir, 1989), especially since it places those who have been made to feel entirely powerless by their abusers (and frequently, also, by the services which intervene once the abuse is suspected or revealed) in direct control of the nature and pace of the work. Whilst the emotional content in such groups clearly needs sensitive handling, there is nothing to suggest that members may not wish, in time, to go beyond this into commenting or taking action on external issues. These may range from medical, police and judicial handling of sexual abuse cases, to the manifest failure of patriarchal society to protect children from being used as sexual objects.

In all the other areas of social services work, too - with disabled people (Heptinstall, 1982), those with learning difficulties, and the parents of these groups - whether black (Jervis, 1986; Sheik, 1986) or white (Cornwell, 1989) - with elderly people (see section on 'Age' in Chapter Two) and users of the mental health services (Randall, 1986) - examples of self-directed groups abound. There has been both local and national campaigning by carers' organisations on matters which directly affect them (Hadley, 1987). An empowering approach can make groups of black and Asian service users less subject to white institutional definitions of what is appropriate, even down to what language should be spoken in the group (Hayre, 1989, pp.22-23). Across all groups of users of social services, then, the approach recommends itself as able to tackle the issues of most concern to users themselves.

Many areas of the health services are equally ripe for change. A team of a health visitor, two nursery nurses and a midwife, for example, is using empowering groups in a terraced house in the heart of the inner city of Nottingham. The team aims to work in partnership with young parents who choose to attend, to help them identify their own health needs, improve the quality of child care and family health by building up self-esteem, offer opportunities to increase practical knowledge and skills, and provide a place to share experiences and learn from one another. Groups run in the house are jointly planned and are encouraged to see the connections between child care issues, women's own personal needs, and their wider role in society. Discussion in a group which began with a focus on parenting skills, for example, ranged over domestic violence, incest and child abuse survival. Another group, for teenage mothers with babies under six months, has arranged and given talks to fourth and fifth year Child Care pupils on a range of subjects and spoken on local radio, all on its own initiative. The skills they already have are recognised and valued in the groups, and this gives them the confidence to acquire new knowledge. Some women now plan to meet in the house each week to take an Open University course and may well progress beyond this. All this has come about through the adoption of a value-base which is quite different from that of the majority of Health Service professionals who tend to see young mothers from deprived areas as hopeless cases who need close surveillance and heavy-handed instruction. It is, therefore, a further aim of the staff to change currently prevailing attitudes and services and to teach new ways of working. They have commented:

> In the last year we have all changed our attitude and approach to parents. We are impressed by the abilities and skills of parents who cope so well under the pressures of poverty, poor housing and limited health opportunities. We see our work as building on these strengths and more importantly doing our best to raise the parents' self-esteem. (Nottingham Health Authority, undated)

Future priorities for the team include the development of a race policy, particularly in relation to children's play activities in the house, dealing with racism, undertaking ethnic monitoring of referrals and group membership, and responding to the needs of mixed race children. They also want to find appropriate ways of working more effectively with fathers.

In the educational services, likewise, the self-directed approach has much to offer. The members of a group for partially hearing adolescents were in their last year at school. The issue here was that their situation was due to change, virtually overnight, from one of tight control and rigid rules at school, to one where resilience and independence are essential for emotional survival as a disabled person in a disabling society. Group members were not prepared passively to 'come to terms' with the limitations which life appeared inevitably to present. Although the group did not run for long enough to take up campaigning, it did fully debate the over-protection of disabled young people in the educational system and then challenged the need for this by organising its own trip to France.

In services for youth, as well as the many examples of empowering work given throughout this book, there are urgent needs in working with unemployed young people (Ward and Harrison, 1989) and with those who turn to drugs or substance abuse (Rogowski et al., 1989).

The statutory sector, then, is ripe for the wide-scale development of self-directed groups to rival the well developed examples in the voluntary sector. Some groups have actually moved from the statutory into the voluntary sector as they have become self-supporting. The North Braunstone Women's Self-Help and Action Group began life as a piece of work instigated by two field workers from a social services' area office with women members who were on the statutory caseloads of workers in the area. It later transferred into the voluntary sector when its members became constituted into the management committee of the new Turning Point Women's Centre. The groupwork model which was used with and by this group also changed over time. Although based on an underlying feminist analysis throughout, at first it was a relatively conventional 'mutual support' group. Later, a community worker became involved and attempted to introduce the ideas of community campaigning. Out of this grew increased awareness and self-confidence on the part of the women group members which eventually saw them transforming the group along true self-directed lines and taking control of its functioning and its future.

Other groups have commenced life, and have remained, in the voluntary sector. The Derbyshire Coalition of Disabled People, for instance, has at all times been run by a management committee of disabled people, and Nottingham Patients' Councils Support Group is one-hundred-per-cent user run. By definition, they are directed by their members but they fall within the model of 'self-directed groupwork' not only for this reason, but also because of the values on which they are constructed. This is not to say that they, or many of the other groups, were set up to be examples of self-directed groupwork. As was explained in Chapter One, the process mainly worked the other way round, in that we studied existing groups first and drew out the model afterwards as a way of disseminating it to other practitioners and activists to help make their work more effective.

RESOURCE RESTRICTIONS

It should never be argued that there is an economy of scale in group, as opposed to individual, work because people can be seen together rather than singly. That would be individual work conducted in parallel, in any case, and not groupwork. Setting up any group is a time-consuming business and, once it is running, there will be planning and feedback meetings to attend as well as the group meetings themselves and any peer support or consultancy arrangements. There may also be recording to do and possibly some individual work continuing alongside the groupwork. Groupwork is demanding and tiring work, with peaks and troughs which can be draining for the worker. It is not to be undertaken lightly, therefore, or in a way which skimps its full potential. Self-directed groupwork does have the tremendous 'highs' of notable achievements to set against all these demands on the worker, but the costs both to the worker and to the agency are still considerable.

On the other hand, self-directed groupwork does have the potential to achieve changes which can release new resources at the local level and it also offers the not inconsiderable secondary advantage of personal change in group members which often far surpasses anything that could be hoped for using traditional approaches. As was mentioned above, the model facilitates partnership even in statutory work, and is also viable in seemingly entrenched and hopeless situations. So, in the last analysis, we may be better advised to enquire whether an agency can afford *not* to allow its use rather than the other way around.

Worker Related Issues

EXPERTISE

Moving on, from potential organisational obstacles to the adoption of the self-directed approach to those which concern workers themselves, readers who have followed us thus far may feel that they would not be skilful enough to put the ideas expressed in this book into practice in their own work. Yet the workers with the groups to which we have referred have not been possessed of extraordinary expertise. On the contrary, they have been ordinary field and residential social workers, teachers, community workers, volunteers, probation officers, Health Service professionals and others, in addition to user activists themselves. They have all been able to play a part in an exciting 'user revolution', not because they are at a pinnacle of skill or ability which cannot be replicated by others, but because they have held firm to the practice principles which were outlined in Chapter Two and found ways to translate these into user-directed action.

Often, they have done so in unsupported circumstances, with colleagues and managers failing to understand what they were proposing. They have not had the benefit of very much published material to turn to, and what there has been has been largely anecdotal. They have, therefore, needed a higher degree of both courage and vision than should henceforth be necessary. Practitioners following after them and reading this book will have the earlier successes reported here to point out to their managers as well worth repeating.

WORKER ATTITUDES

A more profound obstacle than lack of expertise or experience is that of workers' attitudes, particularly where these are in conflict with the values expressed in Chapter Two. When some professionals who are new to the approach hear what members of groups have achieved - that they have set up self-advocacy representation across every geographical sector of a mental health service, for example, or obtained funding for a women's centre and employed their own staff, or spoken at an international conference - there is a fairly stock initial response of 'Oh, the people I work with could never do that'. This betrays the deeply entrenched effect of negative labelling in their world view. Perhaps only good humour and the triumph of factual successes over doubts and scepticism can combat it.

At a recent mental health users' conference, recalling the

early doubts of professionals that Dutch models of patient representation could ever be replicated here, this obstacle of worker perceptions was referred to as the 'They've got a better class of loonies in Holland' argument. A significant number of agencies and their staff assume that only a better class of delinquents could be trusted with their own youth centre, only a better class of black and white youth could run their own music festival, and so on. While ever we believe that 'our mentally handicapped [sic] are worse than yours' we will not believe that the users *we* work with can also interview prospective staff (Brandon, 1987) or express their own views. The same tendency can be observed in opposition to the right of birth mothers to organise campaigning groups in this country, as they have done in New Zealand and Australia, to fight for access to their children and for future policies of open adoption to be developed. It is easy for those professionals who remain to be convinced to argue that the women who organised elsewhere were probably reasonable people who had just been unfortunate, whereas the ones on their own caseloads are inadequate, abusive, and manipulative. It is important to look to Principle 1 to dispel such negative labels, since they block any chance of user-led work.

User Related Issues:
When, and with whom, might the approach not be applicable?

Self-directed groupwork does not supplant traditional groupwork methods but is offered as an alternative which will be more appropriate in many specific instances. In other words, one limitation on its use should be that it will not *always* be the most appropriate way to intervene and should not be applied like a supposed panacea any more than any other approach would be. Much depends on the site of the primary problem - the area in which change is to be sought. If this lies within the individual and their personal functioning, then traditional approaches may be more appropriate, at least to start with, be they problem-solving, psychotherapeutic or group interaction models of groupwork (Brown, 1986, pp.16-19). More frequently in our view, the essential causes of the difficulties - some of which may of course manifest themselves in the behaviour of individuals - may be traced back to the wider community or environment.

There is, of course, no easy yardstick to apply in reaching this judgement. In the past, traditional approaches have been allowed to predominate, either because the individual worker, their managers or agency have not held a value system which would allow for the wider social perspective, or because the worker has not felt equipped - given prevailing methodology and the current inadequate resources and inhospitable political climate - to begin to contemplate change at the macro level. However, when one can take the wider view, even the most unlikely of individuals can join together and seek to bring about wider-scale change through groupwork, particularly if they begin with localised issues and band together with others before considering matters on a national scale. Where this can be attempted, whether the external problem they face is of recent origin or long entrenched, then the self-directed groupwork model is more appropriate than its predecessor approaches. It does not collude with 'blaming the victim' (Ryan, 1971; Elton, 1989, pp.72-73), and it it is capable of attacking the root rather than merely the symptoms of the problems.

INDIVIDUAL CHOICE

Of course, it should not only be the worker who has any say over whether and when self-directed groupwork is the most appropriate method of working. Membership of the groups must always be entirely voluntary or the approach is nullified. It follows, then, that potential group members must have a real choice as to what form of help they prefer. If they do not wish to opt into this, or perhaps any kind of group, there must still be individual professional support available.

We would not wish, however, as we have said elsewhere (Mullender and Ward, 1985, p.171), to countenance individual work which stopped short at an inappropriately individually-focused assessment. Just as empowerment implies moving away from 'blaming the victim' (Ryan, 1971) for his or her own experience of socially created problems, so this victim-blaming tendency should be avoided in individual work. If there is an external reason for that person's problems and if what is really required is external change, then there should be no failure to say so, to the individual concerned or to others, and no easy slipping into seeking to change them instead of the external factor just because they are to hand. This would constitute unwarranted intrusion.

Work which is appropriately undertaken with individuals (or in a group setting but focused on individual change), should also be as transformed by the values of empowerment, as is the groupwork itself. Once a practitioner has recognised the potential for group achievement and personal change that has been demonstrated in self-directed groups, it should, thereafter, never be possible to 'talk down' to any user of the service one is offering, or to fail to inform and involve them in decision-making, or to patronise them as unable or unworthy to reach one's own level of functioning (Satyamurti, 1981, p.524). Beyond this changed style of professional intervention (Keefe, 1980), however, should be added the potential for referring on those individuals who so choose to self-directed groups, once the help they have received *as* individuals has assisted them to feel confident enough, and to be outwardly-focused enough to join. In other words, even where a symptom of wider problems, such as depression, has taken on its own momentum (Wilson, 1980, p.39) and has made it desirable to open the intervention by broaching that issue with the individual, such individual work should not be seen as complete in itself. When it has reached some kind of turning point of success, the person should be asked once more to opt either for more work alone, or for involvement in a group, or for the intervention to end there if they prefer.

There may be several such points of choosing and re-choosing within one whole piece of work, and a number of different combinations of individual, couple, family work, or groupwork, sequentially or in parallel. To sum up this way of conceptualising whole and multi-part pieces of work, we have a shorthand phrase: 'it's not where you start that matters, but where you stop'.

ABILITY TO PARTICIPATE

As with any method, it may be instructive to ask ourselves whether there are any limitations on who can be considered able to participate in, and to benefit from, a self-directed group. Unlike some types of groups, this one could not justly be accused of being confined to those who are already very articulate. Whilst they may be more than able to do so by the time they leave, many members of self-directed groups come to the groups unable even to put their most pressing opinions easily into words, and it is one of the crucial roles of the facilitator to give them a range of opportunities to feel listened to, and to learn the skills to voice their views. A good example of this was the example mentioned in Chapter Four, where a detached youth worker met up with some young people on a street corner, asked them where else they might prefer to meet, and promptly wrote their answers in chalk on the paving stones. Not all of us will have the wit or the flair to offer an instant brainstorm al fresco, but we can all learn the lessons of alert listening, of valuing the user's point of view, and of being innovative when the need arises.

Self-directed groups have as few restrictions on the age of their participants as any method of working. Only those who are too young, or too disabled, to possess the power of communicable thought to any usable degree would actually be ruled out. Groups for children in care have successfully included members as young as ten, and we would not propose even that age as necessarily a minimum. The work at Elton House (Mullender and Ward, 1985) included at least one member who was aged over ninety. Much depends, again, on how skilful and open-minded the group facilitator is able to be.

Similarly, group members do not need to possess the power of comprehensible speech, as the group for deaf young people proved, or of sophisticated abstract conceptualisation, as long as the worker is prepared to help them find other means of considering and putting forward their own views, and of comprehending those of other group members. Non-verbal, pictorial, or activity-based communication can be extremely powerful and effective.

Groups of disabled people have shown that members of self-directed groups do not need to be able to move about unaided, though they fight unendingly for their right to be assisted to do so. Groups in residential settings have further illustrated that it is freedom of thought rather than freedom of physical scope which is essential to a self-directed group.

The Heart of Self-Directed Groupwork

The approach we have presented in this book, when all the obstacles have been overcome and it has flourished in an unparalleled way, has, even then, sometimes been dismissed as 'just community work by another name'. This we would dispute. One of the key aspects of self-directed groupwork which is not shared with community work is its membership. Our model of groupwork has been drawn from groups which have arisen either in statutory settings or amongst specific populations of those who are, or who have been, users of welfare agencies. Being identified as such is what has brought them all together, and we would emphasise that this places self-directed groupwork firmly within the mainstream. Some of the people who have become designated clients and who join self-directed groups are, in fact, individuals for whom social workers hold formal and legal responsibility through statutory orders, as was explored in Chapters Three and Five.

The examples of self-directed groups we have drawn on include elderly people in residential care, young offenders, and parents who have abused their children - none of them groupings with whom community workers have traditionally concerned themselves, but ones whom the other professions listed may well see every week of their working lives and with whom much of the rest of their intervention may be experienced as heavily interventive and unwanted. It is a special problem for them to find ways of managing both their authority role and their facilitative groupwork role but many practitioners do manage this juggling act, even in the heart of the statutory sector.

The question may further arise, in all the examples given in this book, of how to tell whether this juggling act has been managed - how one may distinguish self-directed work from well-intentioned but essentially less empowering practice. The answer lies in the anti-oppressive values, and in the broad social analysis on which they are based - arrived at through asking the question 'WHY' - to which we consequently return full-circle. Groups are not fully empowering if, through the influence of the worker, they stop short at providing only a source of mutual help and support, or at simply lamenting shortfalls or failings in services. Valuable as support may be, it does not help participants to generalise from their particular situation to wider social processes, without which there can be no awareness of the forces of oppression or of the potential for powerless groups to take action to confront them. On the other hand, many groups have the potential to develop from humble beginnings very much further along self-directed lines. We hope that this book will help in that process.

What we have distinguished to offer them, as discrete and essential about self-directed groupwork, is not merely a new configuration of descriptive features or a new menu of techniques, but a clear statement of the values held by both members and practitioners from which their methods of working together flow. In particular, self-directed groups have a distinctive collaborative commitment to achieving social change on issues identified and owned by the group members themselves. Both this commitment and the values from which it springs are a world apart from those to be found, explicitly or implicitly, in most work in the social welfare field.

Looking to the Future

Just as the practice which springs from this recognition is empowering, so can the methods of research and training on empowerment be - but only if, firstly, they fully involve participants in setting their own agendas for relevant goals and non-oppressive processes of discovery or new learning, and, secondly, they seek a broader social analysis through asking the question 'WHY?'. It would, of course, be entirely inappropriate as well as ineffective if the self-directed approach were to be studied or taught in ways which did not reflect this value-base in action. Once again, a framework of basic principles and ways of working needs to be built up, stage by stage, and held in common across disciplines. We have begun this work, both in teaching (Harrison et al., 1982; Ward, 1986; Ward and Mullender, 1988) and in research (Mullender and Ward, 1988), building on the work of learner-directed adult educators (Freire, 1972; Knowles, 1978; Nottingham Androgogy Group, 1983) for the former, and participative research models (Reason and Rowan, 1981), including those which reflect feminist (Stanley and Wise, 1983) and anti-racist (Dutt, 1989) ideals, for the latter.

We offer training workshops which model the techniques of self-directed work, so that participants' own experiences as learners offer them a basis for their future practice with service users (Social Action Training, 1989), whilst our research is aimed at transforming the 'subjects' into full partners. These areas of endeavour, together with the continued refinement and dissemination of the self-directed approach in direct practice, will demonstrate our continuing commitment to empowerment work in the foreseeable future.

Appendix

The best general source of information about self-directed groupwork is **The Centre for Research and Training in Social Action Groupwork, School of Social Studies, University of Nottingham, Nottingham NG7 2RD.** Consultants, trainers, guest speakers and researchers on self-directed groupwork can all be contacted through the Centre.

Group Examples

The major group examples, which recur throughout the book, are summarised here in the order in which they first appear in the text. Contact points are included where appropriate. Many other, briefer examples are also used. Information about any of these may be obtained through the Centre for Social Action at the above address.

Example a: Nottingham 'Who Cares' Group

This was a group for young people of twelve and over, who were in the care of the local authority (both foster care and residential care). The group had two aims: 'to make things better in care' and 'to let people know what care is like'. In addition, the group was affiliated to the National Association of Young People In Care (NAYPIC) and therefore subscribed to its aims including: improving conditions in care and after care; promoting the views and opinions of young people in care; and educating the public on all aspects of the needs and views of young people.

In common with youth social action groups (see the Ainsley example below), the in-care movement is founded on a belief that young people have many capabilities which not only are not seen or tapped by adults, but which are actively denied, particularly where the young person has been given a negative label such as 'young offender' or 'deprived child'. In fact, however, NAYPIC and 'Who Cares' have found that young people who are trusted and given responsibility have an enormous amount to contribute on behalf of all those who are currently in care and those who will follow them. Locally, the Nottingham 'Who Cares' group was instrumental in requesting and preparing a guide for children coming into the care of the local authority, which included an explanation of their rights and what to expect from care. The group also invited the Director and Chair of Social Services to meet with it; was interviewed on the local radio; organised one of the national NAYPIC meetings and a disco to follow; undertook a wide range of fund-raising activities; gave many talks to social work students, to other young people in care, and to foster parents; and made its own video to be used as an ice-breaker at these talks. Although the group folded when many of its members came to the stage of leaving care, it had certainly made its mark over approximately a four year period.

The Nottingham 'Who Cares' Group is no longer running. Questions about it may be addressed to: Audrey Mullender, Centre for Applied Social Studies, Department of Sociology and Social Policy, University of Durham, Elvet Riverside II, New Elvet, Durham DH1 3JT

Example b: Ainsley Teenage Action Group (ATAG)

This started life as a natural (i.e. pre-existing) group of teenagers who had offended together on the council estate where they lived. Their probation officer, along with two other workers, decided that a social action approach would help the young people to work together as a group to improve leisure facilities on the estate, the lack of which had been, in their own view, an important factor in the causation of their offences. The teenagers wanted to recruit friends into the group and the workers agreed, in recognition that they all faced the same external problems on the estate so that it was a false distinction to see pathology in some but not others. This is in marked contrast to traditional groupwork, where workers select the members for the group and the group is then closed.

Once the group was formed and had set goals for itself, the members produced a petition, ran a public meeting, raised funds and approached the council concerning the needs of the estate. The young people used the media, and their own purposeful activities, to challenge the labels of 'delinquent' and 'disruptive' which they had previously borne. In this way, they succeeded in being taken seriously. The method used by the workers placed responsibility on group members, both for decisions and for action. The young people became increasingly able to accept this responsibility and eventually obtained a plot of land for a youth club, a portable building to put on it, and an Inner Area grant for essential services.

The group members went on to review their campaigning and to take up other issues, as is indicated in the later stages of the self-directed groupwork model. One such issue was that of policing practices on the estate. The young people felt that they were being harassed by the police patrolling their estate. They therefore sought and obtained a meeting with the local Chief Inspector, who agreed that he would put different officers on duty there, in return for a guarantee of a less obstructive attitude towards the beat constables. Both sides of this negotiated arrangement were kept to, and the Chief Inspector obtained several large pieces of equipment for the group, spoke favourably about it in a televised interview, and generally became one of the group's firmest supporters.

The group moved on to a process of continuing campaigns, reviews, new issues, and an analysis of underlying injustices towards young people - particularly those who had been in trouble with the police. They came to perceive quite clearly that it was their status as teenagers which brought them unfair treatment, and they built this awareness into their campaigning. An example arose in relation to the management structure of the youth club which they won for the estate: ATAG insisted on keeping this under the control of young people, despite bureaucratic regulations which called for adult supervision.

An interesting postscript on social action work with young people in Nottingham is to report that the parliamentary Select Committee on Children invited another group, which had links with ATAG, to meet with relevant members of the upper and lower Houses at Westminster. The young people's 'user viewpoint' was both confidently offered and well received.

The three original workers with the Ainsley Teenage Action Group are all willing to be contacted to discuss their work. They are:
Colin Butcher, Nottinghamshire Probation Service, 38 Robin Hood Chase, St Anns, Nottingham NG3 4EZ
Mark Harrison and Dave Ward, The Centre for Research and Training in Social Action Groupwork, School of Social Studies, University of Nottingham, Nottingham NG7 2RD

Group Example c: Rowland Dale Group for Parents with Children on the Child Protection Register

NB: The name of this group has been disguised for reasons of confidentiality.

The Rowland Dale Group was formed specifically for the purpose of working in a new way. Unusually, it arose from a worker's theoretical understanding of the problems facing group members and his ideological wish to follow through that understanding into his practice. Hence, the objective of the group was to focus on the physical abuse of children not at the intra-psychic (personal stress or inadequacy) or inter-psychic (family dynamics and relationships) levels, but as the background to tackling the structural pressures that the worker believed were an important factor in causation. This involved:

* focusing on issues such as unemployment, poverty and bad housing,
* looking at the responses of statutory agencies to reports of child abuse, including the formal procedures such as registers and case conferences and the lack of involvement of parents in these,
* encouraging mutual support between members.

The initiating worker recruited two co-workers. Unfortunately, they did not share the same underlying values or aims, with the result that one of the three left after only a short time. This left a social worker and a health visitor to run the group.

The Rowland Dale Group did not fully depart from traditional assumptions about groupwork in that referrals were sought for members, rather than having an open and non-selected membership, and a pre-determined number of meetings was arranged with guest speakers for many of the sessions. This did not allow the members long enough to explore or arrive at their own definition of their situation so they could not begin to define or tackle external goals in the way the initiating worker had originally hoped. Not surprisingly, the original idea of encouraging the members to take over the group after the designated ten sessions was also not feasible in the time available and, after six group meetings run independently by the members, the group folded.

For these reasons, the Rowland Dale Group represents only an early stage in the development of the self-directed model.

Nevertheless, what it did achieve was a radical departure from the tremendous weight of traditional approaches, in all statutory agencies, to the understanding and 'treatment' of child abuse. This was based on a recognition in practice that, very often, structural factors play an important role in causation and that groupwork can potentially provide a way of beginning to tackle them, even in statutory settings. Hence, the Rowland Dale groupworkers played an important part in contributing to the genesis of the model outlined in this book.

Further information about the Rowland Dale Group can be obtained from:
Steve Rogowski, The Centre for Research and Training in Social Action Groupwork, School of Social Studies, University of Nottingham, Nottingham NG7 2RD

Group Example d: North Braunstone Women's Self-Help and Action Group

Two local authority social workers took the first initiative in establishing this group, originally as a way of meeting with a group of mothers whose standards of child care were giving their social workers cause for concern, but using a feminist orientation to put more of the emphasis on the women's own needs and views than would normally have been the case. Typically, the interests of the children would completely have overshadowed the fact that the women were suffering physical violence from their husbands, that they frequently felt 'at the end of their tether', and that there seemed to be nowhere for them on the estate other than the isolation of their own homes. The women grew in confidence and found the company and sharing their experiences with the other women to be invaluable since it helped them to see for the first time that the violence, and the other problems they faced, were not their own fault.

When the two social workers left the group and a community worker became involved, the members had reached the point where they were ready to move beyond merely surviving from day to day, into looking around them at what was wrong with their estate. At first, these wider horizons led to some fairly conventional community work activity, in relation to a traffic proposal. Eventually, however, the group became entirely self-directing in its choice of issues and its ability to put the necessary work into these. The group fought hard to secure a women's centre for the estate, for which they now constitute the management committee. They also now employ their own worker. This has involved not only learning about employment law, contracts, and other technical details, but also moving into a phase of facilitating their worker to work effectively on their behalf rather than being facilitated by her themselves.

This group has made enormous strides over a period of a few years. The women members have reached an understanding of the injustice with which women are treated, and have made the links in their thinking across many areas of their own lives, including in relation to health issues, issues concerning the benefits system, and the safety of women on the streets at night. They have progressed, in both collective and personal terms, to being sufficiently confident to advise other women's groups on how to obtain and run their own centre, and to make a presentation at a national conference of social work educators.

Further information is available from:
Turning Point Women's Centre, 27 Cantrell Road, Braunstone, Leicester LE3 1SD

Group Example e: Asian Society

In response to an urgent call from the local public library to 'do something' about a group of Asian young people who were 'hanging around' and causing a nuisance there, a detached team of Asian youth workers sent one permanent worker and one social work student to meet with the young people concerned. It transpired that they were students at the nearby further education college, who needed to use the library to study in, but who also treated it as something of a social centre where they could meet friends of both sexes, because its educational connotations meant that their parents did not object to their going there. They felt that they actually needed an opportunity to hold meetings of Asian young people at the College, but that neither the staff nor the other students would support this request.

With the help of the two workers, the group did successfully negotiate for a place to meet at the College, during normal timetabled hours. They also raised a number of matters which were of concern to them all with the college authorities, including racist attacks by white students, and the racism embedded in staff attitudes and in the organisation of the college. Within the group itself, the Asian workers were able to use their affinity with the group members to assist them in considering how, as young people, they wanted to be able to meet their friends more freely but how, as Asian young people, they did not want to flout their families' wishes nor the cultural and religious norms of their community.

A further interesting issue arising from the process within the group, was the tension between the male and female members, with the latter saying that the young men did not listen to them and insisting that sexism was as much a problem as racism. After withdrawing to discuss their needs on their own, the young women then returned with a set of proposals which the group eventually accepted. For the future, it was decided that, when the male student social worker left, the remaining male worker should be joined by a female colleague as his co-worker.

Further information about groupwork with young Asian people in the Nottingham area may be obtained from: Project Pehchan, The Asian Detached Youthwork Team, Sneinton Youth and Community Centre, Beaumont Street, Sneinton, Nottingham NG2 4PJ

Group Example f: Derbyshire Coalition of Disabled People (DCDP)

The Coalition's constitutional commitment to be 'of', rather than 'for' disabled people, and its basic definition of disability are central to its work and to its inclusion as an example in this book. The Coalition regards disability as an inevitable by-product of a form of social organisation which takes little or no account of people who have physical, sensory or learning impairments. In other words - and in opposition to those definitions which have emerged out of physically and mentally 'able-bodied' people's perceptions - the Coalition's position is that only the basic *impairment* resides in the individual. He or she is *disabled* by a society which does not make the physical world accessible to people with restricted mobility; which does not routinely teach a range of communication skills to all its citizens, or offer even its official communications in forms which can be understood by all; which requires a large proportion of disabled people to live in poverty, and often closes all employment opportunities to them; but which could, if the holders of power and influence so chose, work to remove stigmatising attitudes, until being in a wheelchair was seen no differently from wearing glasses. This 'social model' turns disability clearly into a political issue, but also into a problem which can be overcome, through collective efforts, even when the underlying, irreversible impairment cannot be removed.

The Coalition does not want 'tea and sympathy', nor for disabled people to be counselled to 'adjust' to their disabilities, nor for the media (and sometimes public bodies) to regard 'brave cripple' stories as their greatest potential contribution to the spread of more positive attitudes. On the contrary, it demands practical steps such as ramps, induction loops, peer counselling services (by disabled people for disabled people), integrated living schemes, and full participation in public decision-making, for example in local government. These changes should be regarded as rights and not as concessions. They need to go hand in hand with education to transform the attitudes both of the public and of health and social services staff - in the latter case so that disabled people are not expected to 'come to terms' with living an institutional or otherwise extremely restricted life.

The Coalition has achieved some enormous successes, particularly in the bringing to fruition of an ambitious scheme to establish the Derbyshire Centre for Integrated Living (DCIL) where advice is available about every aspect of life as a disabled person. DCIL has been launched as a separately constituted body, and DCDP has had the opportunity - or the challenge - of reviewing what remaining functions it can most usefully serve. Its campaigning role has come immediately to the fore because, whereas DCIL has to be non-controversial, DCDP has no such restrictions and can speak out loud and long on behalf of disabled people. DCDP is also in a phase of consolidating the skills and strengths of its members so that they can share in representing the Coalition, including on council committees and in giving talks. Some of the longer-standing members are involved on both a national and an international scale in co-ordinating the views of groups *of* disabled people, and presenting these to government and other public bodies.

At the time of writing, DCDP is facing a major funding crisis. Its members are, however, determined to keep it in operation. The Coalition can be contacted at 117 High Street, Clay Cross, Chesterfield S45 9DZ
Derbyshire Centre for Integrated Living is at: DCIL, Long Close, Cemetery Lane, Ripley, Derbyshire DE5 3HY

Group Example g: Elton House

NB: The name of this residential establishment has been disguised to protect the privacy of its residents.

The officer-in-charge of 'Elton House' elderly people's home began the changes he wanted to bring about by introducing group living arrangements. He altered the physical organisation of the home so that, instead of sitting round the walls staring into space, residents were broken up into small groups, in separate living areas, but with encouragement to make formal and informal links across groups. This meant that people could become more involved in the tasks of daily living and retain their independence to the level of their own abilities.

The philosophy underlying the changes was that old age is simply a chronological fact and should not lead to automatic assumptions about an individual's declining abilities, nor to patronising treatment as if elderly people were overgrown children. The home is now run to meet the needs of residents, not those of the local authority. Residents are asked their opinion of the organisation of the home and are listened to. Thus they have a certain degree of say over their own lives and they also offer support to one another, both factors which are looked for in the statement of values contained within the self-directed model.

Although residents gain a good deal in personal terms at Elton House, they are still by no means in total control of what happens to them. Nor are they involved in general discussion of the way the dominant culture in British society treats its older members. This would happen in the fully fledged self-directed model through a consideration of the question 'WHY?'. We therefore see this example as representing an early stage of the model, arising from the desire to introduce principles of good practice, rather than from any thorough-going theoretical analysis.

The establishment in question cannot be identified here but further information about it may be sought through Audrey Mullender, Centre for Applied Social Studies, Department of Sociology and Social Policy, University of Durham, Elvet Riverside II, New Elvet, Durham DH1 3JT

Group Example h: Nottingham Patient Councils' Support Group (NPCSG)

Nottingham Patient Councils' Support Group was developed following a Dutch model and was the first group of its kind in Britain, though the idea has since spread. Alongside a related organisation, Nottingham Advocacy Group, which provides individual advocacy for users of the mental health services, NPCSG aims to establish ward- or day centre-based meetings (the patients' councils) of service users to voice collective complaints about those services. Where the complaints are not satisfactorily dealt with at ward or centre level, the group seeks to be instrumental in creating channels through which users can negotiate with management, so that the problems can be rectified at the necessary level within the hospital or social services.

Both NPCSG and NAG were originally established by professionals working within the voluntary sector, in conjunction with people who had themselves had occasion to use the mental health services but who were now volunteers and activists. NPCSG is now a one hundred per cent user-led and user-managed body, with just a support group of professionals to offer advice but not direction. NPCSG is, therefore, fully self-directed, in line with the model of groupwork described in this book. After remarkable early successes in establishing a presence in several local psychiatric hospitals and units, NPCSG hit a low patch when some of its most active volunteers became 'burnt out' by the level of work required or needed to be supported by the group through further episodes of mental illness. It is now enjoying a revival of its previous fortunes and energies and has a substantial network of volunteer help.

Both Nottingham Patient Councils' Support Group and Nottingham Advocacy Group can be contacted 9A Forest Road East, Nottingham NG1 4HJ

Group Example i: Nottingham Information Project

Nottingham Information Project is one of a range of groups which meet at Prince's House, all of whom are on the leading edge of user-based projects for people with learning difficulties. The offices at Prince's House were established as a resource centre for a range of groups sharing a clear value-base. This centres on collective working and on the involvement of all people as co-workers, regardless of disability. The group members also have a common objective of campaigning for citizens' rights and for integration in the housing, jobs and educational fields, amongst others.

The main task of the Information Project is to produce *Enable* magazine, a campaigning journal which utilises the varying skills of a wide range of people and gives a voice to many whose views would otherwise not be heard. The magazine is written and illustrated by project co-workers and is an enjoyable and instructive read.

Subscriptions to *Enable* magazine are available through: Nottingham Information Project, Prince's House, 32 Park Row, Nottingham NG1 6GR. Information about this and other groups based at Prince's House is available from the same address.

References

ACW (Association of Community Workers) (1981) *Community Workers' Skills Manual*, London: ACW.

Adams, J. (undated) *Ah-Hah! Seminar !!!*, Toronto, Ontario, Canada: unpublished leaflet.

Ahmed, S., Cheetham, J. and Small, J. (1986) *Social Work with Black Children and Their Families*, London: Batsford.

Alinsky, S.D. (1971) *Rules for Radicals*, New York: Vintage Books (Random House).

Alissi, A.S. (ed.) (1980) *Perspectives on Social Group Work Practice: A Book of Readings*, New York: Free Press.

Arnstein, S.R. (1969) 'A ladder of citizen participation', *Journal of the American Institute of Planners*, July, pp.216-224. [Reproduced in April 1971 in *Journal of the Town Planning Institute*, pp.176-182.]

Badham, B. (ed.) (1989) 'Doing something with our lives when we're inside: self-directive [sic] groupwork in a youth custody centre', *Groupwork*, 2(1) pp.27-35.

Badham, B., Bente, M. and Hall, P. (1988) ' "Nowt to do and always getting into trouble" - the Bulwell Neighbourhood Project: a social action response', *Groupwork*, 1(3) pp.239-251.

Badham, B., Butcher, C. and Fleming, J. (1985) *Statutory agencies and social action: the conflicts and questions*, Nottingham: Nottingham Young Volunteers (unpublished paper).

Badham, B., Craig, R., Ward, D. and Wilson, D. (1989) 'Straight talking - what happened at one of the workshops', *Concern*, Winter, pp.3-4.

Bailey, R. and Brake, M. (1975) *Radical Social Work*, London: Edward Arnold.

Bailis, S., Lambert, S. and Bernstein, S. (1978) 'The legacy of the group: a study of group therapy with a transient membership', *Social Work in Health Care*, 3(4) pp.405-418.

Barker, H. (1986) 'Recapturing sisterhood: a critical look at 'process' in feminist organising and community work, *Critical Social Policy*, Issue 16, pp.80-90.

Barker, I. and Peck, E. (1987) *Power in Strange Places: User Empowerment in Mental Health Services*, 380-384 Harrow Road, London W9 2HU: Good Practices in Mental Health.

BBC (British Broadcasting Corporation) (1981) *Grapevine*, programme 3, London: BBC Community Programmes Unit. [Television programme]

Becker, S. and MacPherson, S. (1986) *Poor Clients*, Nottingham: Nottingham Benefits Research Unit, School of Social Studies, University of Nottingham, NG7 2RD.

Bernstein, S. (1972) 'Values and group work' in Bernstein, S. (ed.) *Further Explorations in Group Work,* London: Bookstall Publications.

Bernstein, S. (ed.) (1972) *Further Explorations in Group Work,* London: Bookstall Publications.

Black is Beautiful: The Black and In Care Newsletter, c/o Nello James Centre, 136 Withington Road, Whalley Range, Manchester M16 8FB.

Blood, P., Tuttle, A. and Lakey, G. (1983) 'Understanding and fighting sexism: a call to men' in Movement for a New Society, *Off Their Backs... and On Our Own Two Feet,* Philadelphia PA 19143: New Society Publishers, 4722 Baltimore Avenue.

Bottoms, A.E. and McWilliams,W. (1979) 'A non treatment paradigm for probation practice', *British Journal of Social Work,* 9(2), pp.159-202.

Bozarth, J.D. (1981) 'The person-centered approach in the large community group' in Gazda, G.M. (ed.) *Innovations to Group Psychotherapy.* Springfield, Illinois, USA: Charles C. Thomas. Second edition.

Brager, G. and Specht, H. (1973) *Community Organising,* New York: Columbia University Press.

Brake, M. and Bailey, R. (eds.) (1980) *Radical Social Work and Practice,* London: Edward Arnold.

Brandon, D. (1987) 'Participation and choice: a worthwhile pilgrimage', *Social Work Today,* 21st December, pp.8-9.

Brandon, D. (1989) 'Better to light a candle than curse the darkness', *Social Work Today,* 9th November, p.36.

Brandon, A. and Brandon, D. (1987) *Consumers as Colleagues,* London: MIND Publications.

Brandon, D. and Brandon, A. (1988) *Putting People First: A Handbook on the Practical Application of Ordinary Living Principles,* London: Good Impressions Publishing.

Breakwell, N. (1989) 'Personal statements, public issues', *Social Work Today,* 9th February, pp.14-15.

Brown, A. (1986) *Groupwork* , Aldershot, Hants.: Gower. Second edition.

Brown, A. (1989) 'Groupwork with a difference: the group "mosaic" in residential and day centre settings' in Helland, O., Kaasa, A. and Leiksett, K. (eds.) *Together,* Oslo: Diakonhjemmets Sosialhogskole, pp.29-48.

Brown, A. and Caddick, B. (1986) 'Models of social groupwork in Britain: a further note', *British Journal of Social Work,* 16(1), pp.99-103.

Brown, A., Caddick, B., Gardiner, M. and Sleeman, S. (1982) 'Towards a British model of groupwork', *British Journal of Social Work* , 12(6), pp.587-603.

Brown, A. and Clough, R. (eds.) (1989) *Groups and Groupings: Life and Work in Day and Residential Centres,* London and New York: Tavistock/Routledge.

Bryan, B., Dadzie, S. and Scafe, S. (1985) *The Heart of the Race: Black Women's Lives in Britain,* London: Virago.

Bryant, M., Coker, J., Estlea, B., Himmel, S. and Knapp, E. (1978) 'Sentenced to social work?', *Probation Journal*, 25(4), pp.110-114.

Burghardt, S. (1982) *The Other Side of Organizing: Resolving the Personal Dilemmas and Political Demands of Daily Practice*, Cambridge MA, USA: Schenkman.

Burley, D. (1982) *Starting Blocks: Aspects of Social Education Group Work with Young People*, Leicester: National Youth Bureau.

Butcher, H., Collis, P., Glen, A. and Sills, P. (1980) *Community Groups in Action: Case Studies and Analysis*, London: Routledge and Kegan Paul.

Campaign for People with Mental Handicaps [CMH] (undated) *Self-Advocacy Pack*, CMH, 12A Maddox Street, London W1R 9PL7 CMH Publications, 5 Kentings, Comberton, Cambs., CB3 7DT, in co-operation with People First of Washington State Advocacy Office.

Campbell, B. (1984) *Wigan Pier Revisited: Poverty and Politics in the Eighties*, London: Virago.

Cashmore, E. and Troyna, B. (eds.) (1982) *Black Youth in Crisis*, London: Allen and Unwin.

CCCS (Centre for Contemporary Cultural Studies) (1982) *The Empire Strikes Back: Race and Racism in 1970s Britain*, London: Hutchinson.

Chamberlin, J. (1988) *On Our Own: Patient-Controlled Alternatives to the Mental Health System*, London: MIND. [Originally published in North America in 1977]

Childright, (1989) 'Child-friendly development?', July/August, 58, pp.8-10.

Cm 849 (1989) *Caring for People: Community Care in the Next Decade and Beyond*, London: HMSO [White Paper].

Cohen, P. (1989) 'Top End Team', *Social Work Today*, 23rd November, p.8.

Cohen, S. (1975) 'It's all right for you to talk: political and sociological manifestos for social action', in Bailey, R. and Brake, M., (eds.) *Radical Social Work*, London: Edward Arnold.

Cornwell, N. (1989) 'Learning through empowerment', *Social Work Today*, 16th November, pp.24-25.

Coyle, G.L. (1939) 'Education for social action' in Lieberman, J. (ed.) *New Trends in Group Work*, New York: Association Press. Reproduced in Alissi, A.S. (ed.) (1980) *Perspectives on Social Group Work Practice: A Book of Readings*, New York: Free Press.

Croft, S. (1989) 'Sharing the wider issues of poverty', in *Social Work Today*, 16th February, p.39.

Croft, S. and Beresford, P. (1987) 'We live here and we know the problems', *Community Care*, 16th July, pp.12-13.

Croft, S. and Beresford, P. (1989a) 'Time for social work to gain new confidence', *Social Work Today*, 13th April, pp.16-18.

Croft, S. and Beresford, P. (1989b) 'User-involvement, citizenship and social policy', *Critical Social Policy*, 26, pp.5-18.

Davies, B. (1979) *In Whose Interests*, Leicester: National Youth Bureau.

Davies, B. and Gibson, A. (1967) *The Social Education of the Adolescent,* London: University of London Press.

Davis, L.E. (ed.) (1984) 'Ethnicity in social group work practice', Special issue of *Social Work with Groups,* 7 (3).

Department of Education and Science (1969) *Youth and Community Work in the 1970s: Proposals by the Youth Service Development Council,* London: HMSO.

Derbyshire Coalition of Disabled People (1986a) *The Quiet Revolution: The Struggle for Full Participation and Equality: A Brief Review of the Background and Work of the Derbyshire Coalition, 1981-1986,* 117 High Street, Clay Cross, Derbyshire: DCDP.

Derbyshire Coalition of Disabled People (1986b) *Welcome to the Coalition,* 117 High Street, Clay Cross, Derbyshire: DCDP.

Dominelli, L. (1988) *Anti-Racist Social Work,* London: Macmillan.

Dominelli, L. (1989) 'White racism, poor practice', *Social Work Today,* 12th January, pp.12-13.

Dominelli, L. and McLeod, E. (1989) *Feminist Social Work,* Basingstoke, Hants. and London: Macmillan.

Donnelly, A. (1986) *Feminist Social Work with a Women's Group,* Norwich: University of East Anglia, Social Work Monograph 41.

Douglas, T. (1976) *Groupwork Practice,* London: Tavistock.

Dourado, P. (1990) 'American dreams come true', *Social Work Today,* 1st March, pp.16-17.

Dutt, R. (1989) 'Griffiths really is a white paper', *Social Work Today,* 23rd November, p.34.

Ellis, S. (1988) *Consumer Participation in Local Authority Residential Care for Older People,* Nottingham: University of Nottingham MA/CQSW Dissertation.

Elton, B. (1989) *Stark,* London: Sphere Books.

Enable magazine, an independent publication for and on behalf of persons with learning difficulties, is available from: The Information Project, Princes House, 32 Park Row, Nottingham NG1 6GR.

Eytle, J. (1985) *Setting up a Black Pensioners Group* (unpublished account). Referred to in Muston and Weinstein (1988), op. cit.

Fine, B., Harris, L., Mayo, M., Weir, A. and Wilson, E. (1985) *Class Politics: An Answer to its Critics,* London: Leftover Pamphlets

Finkelstein, V. (1980) *Attitudes and Disabled People: Issues for Discussion,* New York: World Rehabilitation Fund Inc. Reprinted - London: RADAR, Monograph no.5, International Exchange of Information in Rehabilitation.

Flower, J. (1983) 'Creating a forum', *Community Care,* 21st April, pp.20-21.

Foster-Carter, O. (1987) 'Ethnicity: the fourth burden of black women - political action', *Critical Social Policy,* 20, pp.46-56.

Franklin, L. (1989) 'Planning for children', *Childright,* April, 55, pp.18-19.

Freeman, J. (1970) *The Tyranny of Structurelessness*. [First printed by the women's liberation movement, USA, 1970; reprinted by *Berkeley Journal of Sociology*, 1970; issued as a pamphlet by Agitprop, 1972; and by Leeds Women's Group of the Organisation of Revolutionary Anarchists; reprinted by the Kingston Group of the Anarchist Workers' Association; we have used the Dark Star Press edition, which was "ripped off from the AWA reprint, minus the ORA/AWA additions to the text".]

Freire, P. (1972) *Pedagogy of the Oppressed*, Harmondsworth: Penguin.

Fritze, C. (1982) *Because I Speak Cockney, They Think I'm Stupid*, London: Association of Community Workers.

Frost, N. and Stein, M. (1989) *The Politics of Child Welfare: Inequality, Power and Change*, Hemel Hempstead, Herts.: Harvester Wheatsheaf.

Fullerton, M. (1982) 'Taking the initiative', *Community Care*, 17th June, pp.20-21.

Galinsky, M.J. and Schopler, J.H. (1985) 'Patterns of entry and exit in open-ended groups', *Social Work with Groups*, 8(2), pp.67-80.

Garvin, C. and Reed, B. (eds.) 'Groupwork with Women/Groupwork with Men', *Social Work with Groups*, 6(3/4) [Special double issue].

Gazda, G.M. (ed.) (1981) *Innovations to Group Psychotherapy*. Springfield, Illinois, USA: Charles C. Thomas. Second edition.

GATT-Fly (1983) *Ah-Hah! A New Approach to Popular Education*, Toronto, Ontario, Canada: Between the Lines Press.

Gibson, T. (1979) *People Power*, Harmondsworth: Penguin.

Gilroy, P. (1987) *There Ain't No Black in the Union Jack*, London: Hutchinson.

Goldberg, G. and Elliott, J. (1980) 'Below the belt: situational ethics for unethical situations', *Journal of Sociology and Social Welfare*, 7(4), pp.478-486.

Greengross, S. (1988) 'Advocacy schemes: a way to help residents and staff', *Care Weekly*, 1st March, pp.8-9.

Hadley, J. (1987) 'Communicator, campaigner and carer', *Community Care*, 29th January, pp.20-21.

Hadley, J. (1988) 'Speaking for one and all', *Community Care*, 1st September, pp.14-15.

Hale, J. (1983) 'Feminism and social work practice' in Jordan, B. and Parton, N. (eds.)*The Political Dimensions of Social Work*, Oxford: Basil Blackwell.

Hall, P. (1974) *How to Run a Pressure Group*, London: Dent.

Hallett, C. (1987) *Critical Issues in Participation*, Newcastle-upon-Tyne: Association of Community Workers.

Hanmer, J. and Statham, D. (1988) *Women and Social Work: Towards a Woman-Centred Practice*, London: Macmillan.

Harrison, M. (1982) 'Organisational issues' in Ward, D. (ed.) *Give 'Em a Break: Social Action by Young People at Risk and in Trouble*, Leicester: National Youth Bureau.

Harrison, M., Butcher, C. and Ward, D. (1981) 'Community arts, community action, *Youth in Society,* July, 56, pp.7-8.

Harrison, M., Perry, A. and Ward, D. (1982) *Education for Change,* paper presented at the conference of the International Association of Schools of Social Work, Brighton, August 1982.

Hayre, S. (1989) *Asian Users of the Mental Health Services,* Nottingham: University of Nottingham, MA/CQSW Dissertation.

Heap, K. (1966) 'The groupworker as central person', *Case Conference,* 12(7), pp.20-29.

Heap, K. (1988) 'The worker and the group process: a dilemma revisited', *Groupwork,* 1(1), pp.17-29.

Heaume, C. (1986) Letter to the Editor, *The Silence is Broken: Youth Work with Young Gay Men. Articles Reprinted from "Youth in Society", 1982-1985* , Leicester: National Youth Bureau. [Originally published in *Youth in Society,* June 1984, 91]

Heginbotham, C. (1988) 'Consumerism in care', *Community Care,* 21st April, pp.24-25.

Helland, O., Kaasa, A. and Leiksett, K. (eds.) (1989)*Together,* Oslo: Diakonhjemmets Sosialhogskole, pp.29-48.

Henderson, P. and Thomas, D. (1980) *Skills in Neighbourhood Work,* London: Allen and Unwin.

Henderson, P. and Thomas, D. (eds.) (1981) *Readings in Community Work,* London: Allen and Unwin.

Henry, M. (1988) 'Revisiting open groups', *Groupwork,* 1(3), pp.215-228.

Henry, S. (1981) *Group Skills in Social Work,* Peacock.

Heptinstall, D. (1982) 'Handing back the power', *Community Care,* 1st April, pp.10-12.

Hill, W.F. and Gruner, L. (1973) 'A study of development in open and closed groups', *Small Group Behaviour,* 4(3), pp.355-381.

Hodge, F.J.B. [John] (1985) *Planning for Co-Leadership: A Practice Guide for Groupworkers,* 43 Fern Avenue, Newcastle upon Tyne NE2 2QU: Groupvine.

Hope, A. and Timmel, S. (1984) *Training for Transformation.* Gweru, Zimbabwe: Mambo Press.

Hopson, B. and Scally, M. (1979) *Lifeskills Teaching,* London: McGraw-Hill.

Howlett, D. (1985) 'Asian Ah-Hahs', *GATT-Fly Report: A Periodical on Global Issues of Economic Justice,* November, VI(3), pp.1-3. Published by GATT-Fly, 11 Madison Avenue, Toronto, Ontario, Canada M5R 2S2.

Hudson, A. (1985) 'Feminism and social work: resistance or dialogue?', *British Journal of Social Work,* 15, pp.635-655.

Hudson, A. (1989) 'Changing perspectives: feminism, gender and social work' in Langan, M. and Lee, P. (eds.) *Radical Social Work Today,* London: Unwin Hyman, pp.70-96.

Jeffs, A. and Smith, M. (eds.) (1987) *Youth Work* , London: Macmillan.

Jelfs, M. (1982) *Manual for Action.* London: Action Resources Group.

Jervis, M. (1986) 'Asian Mums fight back', *Social Work Today,* 7th April, p.9.

Jones, M. (1953) *The Therapeutic Community,* New York: Basic Books.

Jonsdottir, G. (1989) 'The challenge of feminism to social work. Theories of incest and groupwork practice with incest survivors as an example' in Helland, O., Kaasa, A. and Leiksett, K. (eds.) *Together,* Oslo: Diakonhjemmets Sosialhogskole, pp.49-91.

Jordan, B. and Parton, N. (eds.) (1983) *The Political Dimensions of Social Work,* Oxford: Basil Blackwell.

Kearney, D. and Keenan, E. (1988) ' "Empowerment" - does anyone know what it means?', *Lynx,* February, 34, pp.3-5.

Keefe, T. (1980) 'Empathy, skill and critical consciousness', *Social Casework,* September, pp.387-393.

Keenan, E. and Pinkerton, J. (1988) 'Social action groupwork as negotiation: contradictions in the process of empowerment', *Groupwork,* 1(3), pp.229-238.

Kent-Baguley, P. (1986) 'The silence broken' in *The Silence is Broken: Youth Work with Young Gay Men. Articles Reprinted from "Youth in Society", 1982-1985* , Leicester: National Youth Bureau.

Kidd, R. and Kumar, K. (1981) 'Co-opting Freire: a critical analysis of pseudo-Freirean adult education', *International Foundation for Development Alternatives Dossier,* July/August, 24, pp.25-40.

Knowles, M. (1978) *The Adult Learner: A Neglected Species,* Houston, USA: Gulf Publishing.

Kreeger, L. (ed.) (1975) *The Large Group.* London: Constable.

Laming, H. and Sturton, S. (1978) 'The development of group work in a social service department' in McCaughan, N. (ed.) *Group Work: Learning and Practice,* London: George Allen and Unwin.

Landau-North, M. and Duddy, S. (eds.) (1985) *Self-Help Through the Looking Glass,* Leicester: Leicester Council for Voluntary Service.

Lane, S. (1986) 'Women and child care: factors influencing social work dealings in women's lives', *British Journal of Social Work,* 16, Supplement, pp.111-123.

Langan, M. and Lee, P. (eds.) (1989) *Radical Social Work Today,* London: Unwin Hyman.

Lewis, D.J. (1988) *Putting Women on the Map: Building an Agenda for Change,* 101-2245 W. Broadway, Vancouver, B.C. V6K 2E4, Canada: Women's Research Centre. [Leaflet]

Lieberman, J. (ed.) (1939) *New Trends in Group Work,* New York: Association Press.

Longres, J.F. and McLeod, E. (1980) 'Consciousness raising and social work practice', *Social Casework,* May, pp.267-276.

Lovett, T., Clarke, C. and Kilmurray, A. (1983) *Adult Education and Community Action: Adult Education and Popular Social Movements,* London: Croom Helm.

Lukes, S. (1974) *Power: A Radical View,* Basingstoke, Hants and London: Macmillan.

Lunn, T.(1989) 'Leavening the lump', *Community Care,* 17th August, pp.13-15.

McCaughan, N. (1977) 'Social group work in the United Kingdom' in Specht, H. and Vickery, A., *Integrating Social Work Methods,* London: George Allen and Unwin.

McCaughan, N. (ed.) (1978) *Group Work: Learning and Practice,* London: George Allen and Unwin.

McCaughan, N. (1985) 'Group work going great guns', *Social Work Today,* 22nd July, pp.16-18.

MacShane, D. (1979) *Using the Media,* London: Pluto Press.

Manor, O. (1989) 'Organising accountability for social groupwork: more choices', *Groupwork*, 2(2), pp.108-122.

Marshall, M. (1987) 'Elderly people: rekindling a community spirit', *Community Care,* 5th February, pp.10-11.

Martin, P.Y. and Shanahan, K.A. (1983) 'Transcending the effects of sex composition in small groups', in Garvin, C. and Reed, B. (eds.) 'Groupwork with Women/Groupwork with Men', *Social Work with Groups,* 6(3/4), pp.19-32.

Mistry, T. (1989) 'Establishing a feminist model of groupwork in the probation service', *Groupwork,* 2(2), pp.145-158.

Mitchell, G. (1989) 'Empowerment and opportunity', *Social Work Today,* 16th March, p.14.

Moseley, J. (1987/88) 'The Friday afternoon syndrome: a different approach to Section 1 spending', *Family Rights Group Bulletin,* Winter, pp.6-7.

Movement for a New Society (1983) *Off Their Backs . . . and On Our Own Two Feet,* Philadelphia PA 19143: New Society Publishers, 4722 Baltimore Avenue.

Moyer, B. and Tuttle, A. (1983) 'Overcoming masculine oppression in mixed groups' in Movement for a New Society, *Off Their Backs . . . and On Our Own Two Feet,* Philadelphia PA 19143: New Society Publishers, 4722 Baltimore Avenue.

Mullender, A. (1979) 'Drawing up a more democratic contract', *Social Work Today,* 13th November, pp.17-18.

Mullender, A. (1989-90) 'Groupwork as a response to a structural analysis of child abuse', *Children in Society,* 3(4), pp.345-362.

Mullender, A. (undated) *North Braunstone Women's Self Help Action Group,* unpublished account.

Mullender, A. and Ward, D. (1985) 'Towards an alternative model of social groupwork', *British Journal of Social Work,* 15, pp.155-172.

Mullender, A. and Ward, D. (1988) 'What is practice-led research into groupwork?' in Wedge, P. (ed.) *Social Work - A Third Look at Research into Practice: Proceedings of the Third Annual JUC/ BASW Conference. London, September, 1987*, Birmingham: BASW.

Mullender, A. and Ward, D. (1989) 'Challenging familiar asumptions: preparing for and initiating a self-directed group', *Groupwork*, 2(1), pp.5-26.

Muston, R. and Weinstein, J. (1988) 'Race and groupwork: some experiences in practice and training', *Groupwork*, 1(1), pp.30-40.

National Youth Bureau (1981) *Enfranchisement: Young People and the Law - An Information Pack for Youth Workers*, Leicester: NYB.

NCVS (Nottingham Council for Voluntary Service) (1989) *A Working Definition of Oppression*, Nottingham: NCVS. [Unpublished handout]

Nicholls, J., O'Hara, W., Trotman, A., Roberts, J. and S., Shaban, N., Young People from the Link Unit, Minihane, S., David, G., MacCallum, S. (1985) *A Celebration of Differences: A Book by Physically Handicapped People*, Bristol Broadsides (Co-op) Ltd., 108C Stokes Croft, Bristol BS1 3RU.

Nottingham Andragogy Group (1983) *Towards a Developmental Theory of Andragogy*, Nottingham: University of Nottingham, Department of Adult Education.

Nottingham Health Authority (undated) *45 Cope Street.*

Nottingham Patients Councils Support Group (1989) *Information Pack*, NPCSG, Kilbourn Street, Nottingham NG3 1BQ.

Oliver, M. (1983) *Social Work with Disabled People*, Basingstoke, Hants. and London: Macmillan.

Page, M. (1983) 'Language and community politics - or exorcising the old ideal!', *Talking Points*, 42, London: Association of Community Workers.

Page, R. and Clark, G.A. (1977) *Who Cares? Young People In Care Speak Out*, London: National Children's Bureau.

Parnes, M. (ed.) (1986) *Innovations in Social Group Work: Feedback from Practice to Theory*, New York: Haworth Press.

Parton, N. (1985) *The Politics of Child Abuse*, Basingstoke, Hants. and London: Macmillan.

Pernell, R.B. (1986) 'Empowerment and social group work' in Parnes, M. (ed.) *Innovations in Social Group Work: Feedback from Practice to Theory*, New York: Haworth Press.

Phillipson, C. (1982) *Capitalism and the Construction of Old Age*, Basingstoke, Hants. and London: Macmillan.

Pike, E. (undated) *Empowerment: Personal and Political Change*, 4722 Baltimore Avenue, Philadelphia PA 19143: Movement for a New Society. [First published as an issue of *Creative Simplicity* in October, 1977.]

Pitts, J. (1990) *Working with Young Offenders*, Basingstoke, Hants. and London: Macmillan.

Preston-Shoot, M. (1987) *Effective Groupwork*, Basingstoke, Hants and London: Macmillan.

Preston-Shoot, M. (1988) 'A model for evaluating groupwork', *Groupwork*, 1(2), pp.147-157.

Preston-Shoot, M. (1989) 'Using contracts in groupwork', *Groupwork*, 2(1), pp.36-47.

Ragg, N. (1977) *People Not Cases*, London: Routledge and Kegan Paul.

Randall, L. (1986) 'Some women I know: groupwork in a psychiatric setting', *Social Work Today*, 18th August, pp.16-17.

Reason, P. and Rowan, J. (eds.) (1981) *Human Inquiry: A Sourcebook of New Paradigm Research*, Chichester: John Wiley and Sons.

Rhule, C. (1988) 'A group for white women with black children', *Groupwork*, 1(1), pp.41-47.

Richardson, A. (1983) *Participation*, London: Routledge and Kegan Paul.

Rogowski, S., Harrison, L. and Limmer, M. (1989) 'Success with glue sniffers', *Social Work Today*, 26th October, pp.12-13.

Rogowski, S. and McGrath, M. (1986) 'United we stand up to pressures that lead to abuse', *Social Work Today*, 26th May, pp.13-14.

Rojek, C., Peacock, G. and Collins, S. (1988) *Social Work and Received Ideas*, London: Routledge.

Rowbotham, S., Segal, L. and Wainwright, H. (1979) *Beyond the Fragments: Feminism and the Making of Socialism*, London: Merlin.

Ryan, W. (1971) *Blaming the Victim*, London: Orbach and Chambers.

Sang, B. and O'Brien, J. (1984) *Advocacy: The UK and American Experiences*, London: King Edward's Hospital Fund for London, Project Paper no. 51.

Satyamurti, C. (1981) 'Clients aren't people', *New Society*, 25th June, p.524.

Shardlow, S. (1989) ' Changing social work values: an introduction' in Shardlow, S., *The Values of Change in Social Work*, London: Routledge.

Sheik, S. (1986) 'An Asian mothers' self-help group' in Ahmed, S., Cheetham, J. and Small, J., *Social Work with Black Children and Their Families*, London: Batsford.

Shulman, A.K. (1979) *Burning Questions*, London: Andre Deutsch.

Sivanandan, A. (1982) 'From resistance to rebellion: Asian and Afro-Caribbean struggles in Britain, *Race and Class*, XXIII, pp.111-152.

Smale, G. (1977) *Prophecy, Behaviour and Change*, London: Routledge and Kegan Paul.

Smith, J and Pearse, M. (1986) *Community Groups Handbook*, London: Community Projects Foundation.

Smith, M. (1980) *Creators Not Consumers*, Leicester, National Association of Youth Clubs.

Smith, M. (1981) *Organise!*, Leicester, National Association of Youth Clubs.

Social Action Training (1989) *Social Action Training Pack*, Nottingham: University of Nottingham, School of Social Studies, Centre for Social Action Groupwork.

Stanley, L. and Wise, S. (1983) *Breaking Out: Feminist Consciousness and Feminist Research,* London: Routledge and Kegan Paul.

Stiefel, M. and Pearse, A. (1982) 'UNRISD's [United Nations Research Institute for Social Development] popular participation programme: an inquiry into power, conflict and social change', *Assignment Children,* vol. 59/60, pp.145-162.

Stock Whitaker, D. (1975) 'Some conditions for effective work with groups', *British Journal of Social Work,* 5(4), pp.423-439.

Svedin, A.-M. and Gorosch-Tomlinson, D.(1984) 'They said we didn't exist...', *Social Work Today,* 2nd April, 15(30), pp.14-15.

Taylor, A. and Kemp, T. (undated) *The Transaction Pack,* London: Apex Trust.

Taylor, T. (1984) 'Anti sexist work with young males', *Youth and Policy,* 9, pp.8-16.

Thomas, D. (1986) *White Bolts, Black Locks: Participation in the Inner City,* London: George Allen and Unwin.

Timms, N. (1983) *Social Work Values: An Enquiry,* London: Routledge and Kegan Paul.

Tingle, N. (1989) 'News from the Grandparents' Federation', *Family Rights Group Bulletin,* Spring, pp.23-24. [Contact address: Noreen Tingle, 78 Cook's Spinney, Harlow, Essex CM20 3BL]

Tonkin, B. (1988), 'What the boys in the backroom will have', *Community Care,* 7th April, pp.14-16.

Twelvetrees, A. (1982) *Community Work,* Basingstoke, Hants and London: Macmillan.

Union of the Physically Impaired Against Segregation (1976) *Fundamental Principles of Disability,* London: UPIAS and the Disability Alliance.

Ward, D. (1979) 'Working with young people: the way forward', *Probation Journal ,* 26(1), pp.2-8.

Ward, D. (1982a) 'An alternative approach: theoretical considerations' in Ward, D. (ed.)*Give 'Em a Break: Social Action by Young People at Risk and in Trouble,* Leicester: National Youth Bureau.

Ward, D. (ed.) (1982b) *Give 'Em a Break: Social Action by Young People at Risk and in Trouble,* Leicester: National Youth Bureau.

Ward, D. (1986) 'Radford adds new benefit to a training partnership', *Social Work Today,* 1st September, pp.8-9.

Ward, D. (1987) *The Ainsley Teenage Action Group,* Nottingham: Nottingham Young Volunteers. [Unpublished group account]

Ward, D. and Harrison, M. (1989) *Self-Organised Employment Initiatives and Young People: A Social Action Approach.* Paper presented at an International Workshop on the Self-Help Idea and on the Outlook for Co-operatives, University of Bielefeld, West Germany, April, 1989.

Ward, D. and Mullender, A. (1988) 'The centrality of values in social work education', *Issues in Social Work Education,* 8(1), pp.46-54.

Webb, D. (1985) 'Social work and critical consciousness: rebuilding orthodoxy', *Issues in Social Work Education*, 5(2), pp.89-102.

Wedge, P. (ed.) (1988) *Social Work - A Third Look at Research into Practice: Proceedings of the Third Annual JUC / BASW Conference. London, September, 1987*, Birmingham: British Association of Social Workers.

Williams, P. and Shoultz, B. (1982) *We Can Speak for Ourselves: Self-Advocacy by Mentally Handicapped People*, London: Souvenir.

Wilson, E. (1980) 'Feminism and social work' in Brake, M. and Bailey, R. (eds.) *Radical Social Work and Practice*, London: Edward Arnold.

Wilson, J. (1987) 'Helping groups to grow', *Community Care*, 2nd July, pp.20-21.

Wilson, J. (1988) 'When to let go', *Community Care*, 26th May, pp.34-35.

Wilson, M. (1989) ' A solution from the streets of Top End', *Social Work Today*, 14th December, pp.14-15.

Wilson, V. (1988) 'Participation', *Youth Social Work Mailing*, no. 6, March, pp.12-15.

Wise, S. (1986) *Doing Feminist Social Work: An Annotated Bibliography and Introductory Essay*, Manchester: University of Manchester, Department of Sociology.

Woodrow, P. and Terry, S. (1979) 'Introduction' in The Training/Action Affinity Group of Movement for a New Society, *Building Social Change Communities*, Philadelphia PA 19143: Movement for a New Society, 4722 Baltimore Avenue.

Wright, M. (1985) 'Mirror of a womens group' in Landau-North, M. and Duddy, S. (eds.) *Self-Help Through the Looking Glass*, Leicester: Leicester Council for Voluntary Service.

Wright Mills, C. (1970) *The Sociological Imagination*, Harmondsworth: Penguin.

Youth in Society (1986) 'Comment' in *The Silence is Broken: Youth Work with Young Gay Men. Articles Reprinted from "Youth in Society", 1982-1985* , Leicester: National Youth Bureau. [Originally published in *Youth in Society*, June 1984, 91]

Author Index

Subject Index